Presidential Doctrines:
National Security from Woodrow Wilson to George W. Bush

PRESIDENTIAL DOCTRINES:
NATIONAL SECURITY FROM WOODROW WILSON TO GEORGE W. BUSH

ROBERT P. WATSON,
CHARLES GLEEK AND MICHAEL GRILLO
EDITORS

Nova Science Publishers, Inc.
New York

Senior Editors: Susan Boriotti and Donna Dennis
Coordinating Editor: Tatiana Shohov
Office Manager: Annette Hellinger
Graphics: Wanda Serrano and Matt Dallow
Editorial Production: Maya Colmbus, Vladimir Klestov,
  Matthew Kozlowski and Lorna Loperfido
Circulation: Ave Maria Gonzalez, Vera Popovic, Sean Corkery, Raymond Davis,
  Melissa Diaz, Magdalena Nuñez, Marlene Nuñez and Jeannie Pappas
Communications and Acquisitions: Serge P. Shohov

Library of Congress Cataloging-in-Publication Data

Presidential doctrines: national security from Woodrow Wilson to George W. Bush / Robert P. Watson, Charles Gleek and Michael Grillo, editors.
  p. cm.
Includes bibliographical references (p.) and index.
  ISBN: 1-59033-812-X (hardcover)
  1. National security—United States—History—20th century. United States—Defenses. 3. United States—Military policy. 4. United States—Foreign relations—20th century. I. Watson, Robert P., 1962- II. Gleek, Charles. III. Grillo, Michael.

UA23 .P684 2003
327.73'009'04—dc22   2003015866

Copyright © 2003 by Nova History Publications, An Imprint of
  Nova Science Publishers, Inc.
  400 Oser Ave, Suite 1600
  Hauppauge, New York 11788-3619
  Tele. 631-231-7269   Fax 631-231-8175
  e-mail: Novascience@earthlink.net
  Web Site: http://www.novapublishers.com

All rights reserved. No part of this book may be reproduced, stored in a retrieval system or transmitted in any form or by any means: electronic, electrostatic, magnetic, tape, mechanical photocopying, recording or otherwise without permission from the publishers.

The publisher has taken reasonable care in the preparation of this book, but makes no expressed or implied warranty of any kind and assumes no responsibility for any errors or omissions. No liability is assumed for incidental or consequential damages in connection with or arising out of information contained in this book.

This publication is designed to provide accurate and authoritative information with regard to the subject matter covered herein. It is sold with the clear understanding that the publisher is not engaged in rendering legal or any other professional services. If legal or any other expert assistance is required, the services of a competent person should be sought. FROM A DECLARATION OF PARTICIPANTS JOINTLY ADOPTED BY A COMMITTEE OF THE AMERICAN BAR ASSOCIATION AND A COMMITTEE OF PUBLISHERS.

Printed in the United States of America

For Isabella, who was born about the time this book was published.
Robert P. Watson

For Cher, Kiera, and Gwenn, their love and beauty continue to amaze me.
Charles Gleek

For Vincent and JoAnn for making numerous sacrifices toward my education.
Michael Grillo

Contents

Preface		ix
Introduction		1
Chapter 1	On the History and Use of Presidential Doctrines *Robert P. Watson*	7
Chapter 2	Woodrow Wilson: A Tradition of Internationalism in American Foreign Policy *Charles Gleek*	25
Chapter 3	Harry S. Truman and the Legacy of Containment *Michael Grillo*	41
Chapter 4	The Nixon Doctrine: A New Approach to the Containment Strategy *Richard Yon*	59
Chapter 5	The Carter Doctrine and National Security: An Examination of American Idealism *Melissa Buehler*	77
Chapter 6	The Axis and the Empire: Fighting Evil in the Reagan and Bush Administrations *Mark Warner*	95
Conclusion		113
Appendix A	Presidents	119
Appendix B	Presidential Doctrines	121
Appendix C	U.S. Wars (Declared)	125
Appendix D	Presidential Use of Military Force (not Including Declared Wars)	127
Bibliography		135
Contributors		139
Index		141

PREFACE

The terrorist attacks against the United States on 11 September 2001 prompted a president, who had until then largely been disinterested in international affairs, to a new level of commitment to foreign policy. So too did the tragedy renew American awareness of the precarious state of national security, even in the post-Cold War era. As has often happened in American history, the events also occasioned a new approach to national security policy, conceived in the specific threat, fashioned by the international environment, and reflecting the president's world view and ideological orientation.

As is the case of the events (threats) themselves, the national security response they foster is often so dramatic that it comes to define the presidency of its maker, influence affairs far beyond America's borders, and dictate U.S. foreign and national security policy for years to come. Shifts in U.S. national security thinking of this magnitude are referred to as *presidential doctrines*. Often, these doctrines – axioms that bear the president's name – have been delivered in a major address by the president such as a speech to a joint session of Congress. The first presidential doctrine was announced by President James Monroe on 2 December 1823 during his seventh annual message to Congress. An international version of this phenomenon would be Winston Churchill's "Iron Curtain" speech. Such was the case when President George W. Bush addressed the nation in the immediate aftermath of the 9/11 terrorist attacks.

The Bush administration's response to the threat of international terrorism – whether or not it will prove to be effective and appropriate – signals another important occurrence in the evolution and development of U.S. national security policy. A new threat facing the United States was identified, policy was formulated, and U.S. resources were mobilized to address the threat. At the time of this writing, we are witnessing a new presidential doctrine to guide national security policy. Moreover, although we are still in the early stages of the war against international terrorism, the "Bush Doctrine" appears to mark a significant departure from previous doctrines. Indeed, even the collective security apparatus and thinking that had come to define U.S. policy for a half century prior to the terrorist strikes against the World Trade Center and Pentagon is being reoriented around new overarching principles for national security. Bush's response to the new threat has resulted in the largest reorganization of government since FDR, the creation of new national security organizations (Homeland Security), two wars (Afghanistan and Iraq), tensions among such established allies as France and Germany, and questions about the centrality of NATO and the United Nations in the calculus of U.S. national security decision making.

Accordingly, important questions are being raised.

- What is the Bush Doctrine and is it the appropriate response to security threats?
- How will it impact the conduct of American foreign policy and international affairs?
- Does the Bush Doctrine chart a new course for U.S. national security policy?
- Or, is it simply the logical continuation of past presidential doctrines?
- How have earlier presidential doctrines been formulated and why?
- Are there similarities and differences among the presidential doctrines of the twentieth century and how does the Bush Doctrine compare to them?

Clearly, the Bush Doctrine is worthy of scholarly attention.

The genesis of this book project dates to a graduate seminar on the presidency taught at Florida Atlantic University during the fall of 2002 when George W. Bush's *National Security Strategy of the United States* (which formulates the Bush Doctrine) was released. The aforementioned questions were posed to a group of graduate students who began thinking about the historical importance of presidential doctrines, continuity in U.S. national security policy, and how, why, and under what circumstances such doctrines are crafted. In a test-run of the results of such analysis, a version of what would become this book was presented at the annual meeting of the Western Social Science Association in 2003 in Las Vegas.

Surprisingly, insufficient research has been devoted to comparing presidential doctrines and exploring the historical trends and continuity among them. This book offers a preliminary study of these research questions. It features case studies of several of the most important presidential doctrines of the twentieth century. Not all doctrines and not all presidents of the twentieth century are included for reasons of brevity. Yet, those selected reflect significant challenges to and changes in the direction of U.S. national security policy. The international, security, and political conditions surrounding the formulation of each doctrine are examined and consideration is given to the historical continuity of national security policy and comparisons between the particular presidential doctrine and George W. Bush's National Security Strategy and war on terrorism.

Although *Presidential Doctrines: National Security from Woodrow Wilson to George W. Bush* is not intended to be the definitive source on the topic, readers will find it to be a concise, highly readable, and introductory examination of presidential national security doctrines. The editors and contributors believe that students at all levels as well as those readers with an interest in the American presidency and national security will find the book easily accessible and informative. It is designed to be a supplemental textbook for undergraduate and graduate courses on the presidency, U.S. foreign policy, national security, and related topics. Introductory essays provide an overview and brief history of the topic of presidential doctrines and U.S. national security policy. The book also features appendixes containing helpful resources for the study of presidential national security doctrines.

In putting this book together, the editors and contributors would like to acknowledge a number of colleagues. Thank you to Dr. David Rausch of West Texas A&M University, the organizers and coordinators of the Western Social Science Association annual meeting in 2003, Dr. Jeffrey Morton, Dr. Kenneth Osgood, Dr. Anita Pritchard, Dr. Mark Scroggins, and the Department of Political Science at Florida Atlantic University. The editors wish to also thank Melissa Buehler, Mark Warner, and Richard Yon.

The topic of presidential national security doctrines is important and one we find compelling. It is our hope that readers share our enthusiasm for taking a closer look at these important documents and come away from the endeavor with new insights on them and an appreciation for the challenges presidents face in formulating national security.

Robert P. Watson
Charles Gleek
Michael Grillo

INTRODUCTION

Political scientists, historians, and other social scientists embrace the study of American foreign policy in order to understand how, why, and in what context foreign policy decisions are carried out. Not surprisingly, there is a large body of scholarship that focuses on American foreign policy. At universities around the world, courses are dedicated to the examination of American foreign policy, and numerous panels at professional academic conferences are dedicated to presenting new and pertinent ways of studying U.S. foreign policy.[1] Implicitly, there seems to be an awareness that the topic – especially the area of national security policy – is worthy of advanced study, that foreign policy decision making is a complex and dynamic undertaking, and that foreign polices adopted and promoted by the United States have profound influences around the world.

The study of foreign policy and national security involves both praise and criticism of the actions of the nations and actors who formulated them. Historians who specialize in the field of diplomatic history examine documents, communications, and personal narratives in order to better explain policies and the events that shaped them. Political scientists utilize theories and scientific models

---

[1] For students interested in studying American foreign policy have a wide range of sources from which to draw from. While a simple listing of relevant authors would prove impossible, students can begin by examining the "History of American Foreign Policy" works of Stephen Ambrose, Noam Chomsky, John Lewis Gaddis, George Kennan, Walter LaFeber, Bradford Perkins, David Schmidtz, and William Williams; in addition to the works cited by the authors at the end of each chapter in this text. In addition, academic journals such as *Diplomatic History, International Studies Quarterly, Political Science Quarterly, American Diplomacy* and *International Affairs,* as well as journal databases such as *JSTOR* and other electronic social science collections provide access to a tremendous wealth of scholarly articles. Private organizations and think tanks such as the Foreign Policy Association, the Council on Foreign Relations, and the Brookings Institution offers in-depth analysis of foreign policy issues on their respective web

to identify trends and test hypotheses about the explanations of the what, why, and how of American foreign policy. One conclusion that becomes immediately clear from all of these diverse topics of scholarship is the value of the large body of interdisciplinary discourse that surrounds the study of American foreign policy and national security.

There are many elements of and questions pertaining to foreign and national security policy that one can study. The behavior of organizations that make up the larger defense establishment in the United States are often the focus of academic scrutiny. In this field, theories about how organizations behave are tested against real world events. Decision-making and policy development processes across government sectors and among individuals are also examined. Rational choice models of decision-making are employed to see how, when, and why particular leaders and governments make their decisions. Connections between U.S. economic interests and security objectives, particularly since the 1970s, are also regularly the focus of scrutiny by foreign policy scholars. It is the intention of the contributors to this text to add to the larger body of scholarship by focusing on the history and development of presidential doctrines on foreign policy and national security.

A Brief History of Presidential Doctrines

A doctrine is defined as a principle that embodies a particular set of beliefs, or a statement of policy that is particularly important in the field of international relations.[2] For this text, the notion of a presidential doctrine refers to a presidential statement that defines the foreign policy objectives of the United States for that president's particular administration. A presidential doctrine thus reflects the presidential administration's values, theoretical beliefs, and worldview, as well as a basic guide for how the government is to act internationally over the life of the administration.

---

[2] sites. Finally, periodicals such as *Foreign Policy* and *Foreign Affairs* provide professional assessment of American foreign policy decisions and global events.
From Merriam-Webster's Dictionary, online search, 24 May 2003, <http://www.m-w.com/cgi-bin/dictionary?book=dictionary&va=doctrine>

THE FIRST PRESIDENTIAL DOCTRINES

Doctrines have been an important part of American foreign policy. The earliest presidential doctrine comes from the first American president, George Washington. In his farewell address of 1796, Washington advocated that the United States continue in honest relationships with other countries while preserving the flexibility and independence of the American government in international affairs.[3] He warned against entangling alliances (Washington advised his countrymen to "steer clear of permanent alliances"), advocated solid neutrality toward other powers, and praised the merits of national self-sufficiency. In short, Washington established overarching principles for the conduct of presidents and policy, much as recent presidents would in their doctrines.[4]

The first presidential statement to be labeled as a doctrine was the Monroe Doctrine.[5] Formulated by Secretary of State John Quincy Adams in 1823, the Monroe Doctrine established the United States as the principle power in the Western Hemisphere. The Monroe Doctrine declared that the states of Europe, principally England, Spain, France, and Germany, were to refrain from extending their colonial passions and political activities into the Western Hemisphere. By prohibiting European states from intervening in Latin America, the Monroe Doctrine laid the foundation for all future U.S. foreign policy.

INTERNATIONALISM IN THE TWENTIETH CENTURY

Towards the end of the nineteenth century and into the early twentieth century, the governments in many Latin American countries began to destabilize because of various economic and political problems. In the decades since the invocation of the Monroe Doctrine, the United States consistently intervened to protect American interests in the various countries of Latin America.[6] For instance, the United States frequently used diplomatic and military pressure to establish American supremacy in Latin America, promote American trade, and further exclude European states from economic opportunities in the region.

---

[3] For the text of Washington's address, see <http://www.yale.edu/lawweb/avalon/washing.htm>
[4] Richard Norton Smith, *Patriach: George Washington and the New American Nation* (New York: Houghton Mifflin, 1993), 279.
[5] For a list of important presidential doctrines, see Appendix B.
[6] See Appendix D for a comprehensive list of American military intervention into Latin America during the nineteenth century.

The Spanish-American War, fought in 1898, marked a turning point in American participation in global affairs. Following the war, the international prestige of Spain declined. Spain's principle colony in the Caribbean, Cuba, came under the control of the United States, while U.S. influence began to usurp the former empire in the Philippines and Pacific. In addition, for the first time in its history the United States entered the assembly of states wielding international prowess. This prowess, along with the inability of any European state to extend influence across the Atlantic, allowed the United States to gain supremacy in Latin America's political, economic, and military affairs.

The 1904 Roosevelt Corollary to the Monroe Doctrine represents the second major American presidential doctrine and marks the formation of one of the first national security "regimes" in the United States. The Roosevelt Corollary further defined the values and interest of the United States in Latin America. In addition to excluding European states form the hemisphere, the Roosevelt Corollary established the principle that the United States would reserve the right to use force, if necessary, to protect its economic and political interests in Latin America. The Roosevelt Corollary would come to guide American foreign policy in the Western Hemisphere for much of the first half of the twentieth century.

In a little over one hundred years, the United States had come to develop a set of principles that characterized its participation in international affairs – the establishment of a complex relationship, neither dependent nor independent of European states, and a dominant position in Latin America. The United States engaged in a variety of mechanisms to support these values including diplomatic engagement, economic pressure, and military force. As the twentieth century emerged, the values of American foreign policy, expressed through two presidential doctrines, was to have a profound effect on the world at large. Subsequent doctrines in response to crises such as world war, Soviet expansion, and nuclear threats would build upon the foundation of these early doctrines.

THE APPROACH OF THIS BOOK

This text was written for students and readers lacking advanced study or expertise in foreign policy, the American presidency, and diplomatic history. The book is meant to introduce readers to the basic concepts behind the formulation of national security policy and foreign policy. The following chapters explore the role of presidential doctrines in national security and foreign policy, and include five doctrine-specific case studies. Each case study takes a comparative approach to presidential doctrines, comparing a particular presidential doctrine to the

National Security Strategy of the United States developed by the administration of President George W. Bush. By highlighting the major themes in different presidential doctrines, each case study attempts to link these themes to current and previous American foreign policy guidelines. By showing the linkage and development of these common themes, the cases are able to show a certain level of continuity in American foreign policy values over the last century despite varying threats and international circumstances.

The cases also include historical study relating to the field of American foreign policy. The field of diplomatic history if often divided into different historical frames. A historical frame provides guidelines and general assumptions for those who seek to explain particular events. While not as specific as a scientific theory, which tests hypothesis and assumptions against actual events, a historical frame is no less valid or important to social science scholars.

There are three principal historical frames in which American foreign policy is often studied. Orthodox historians perpetuate traditional accounts of American history. Examples of this frame include the validity of manifest destiny and concept of American isolationism. Despite the name "orthodox," which often refers to primary or conventional, orthodox historians simply reflect a particular set of ideas about the history of American foreign policy. Revisionist historians, originating from the Wisconsin School of thought during the 1960s, challenge the assumptions and accounts of orthodox historians. Often arguing that economic motives played a leading role in formulating American foreign policy, revisionist historians offered new and important accounts of issues ranging from American westward expansion to the establishment of an American Empire. Post-revisionist historians seek to develop a synthesis between the views and accounts of both orthodox and revisionist historians. While accepting some of the revisionist assumptions and factual explanations for American motives in foreign policy, particularly those that incorporate economic motives and details, post-revisionists often reinforce traditional accounts for historical events. Within this complex array of scholarship, students should understand that there is not necessarily a singular account of history. It is important to appreciate the strengths and weaknesses of each historical frame.[7]

In this text, the authors tended to refrain from adopting any one particular frame of reference for the historical evidence utilized in the case studies. Since our aim was to provide a general overview of presidential doctrines for undergraduate students, the lack of a consistent historical frame seems to make

---

[7] For a cogent and detailed explanation of historical study and U.S. foreign policy, see Jerel A. Rosati, *The Politics of United States Foreign Policy*, 2nd Ed. (Fort Worth, T.X.: Harcourt Brace College Publishers, 1999), 20.

the most sense. Presenting information from only one historical perspective has the tendency to marginalize other relevant points of view. Consequently, much of this work can be categorized as reflecting the orthodox historical view of American foreign policy. This is not a value judgment of a particular course of study, or an endorsement of particular set of beliefs. Rather, the historical accounts reflected in this work were written in such a way as to be easily disseminated by students, new to this subject. Without deviling into epistemological debates about the nature of historical inquiry and political discourse, the authors would, rather, encourage discussion amongst the readership about the different ideas and themes presented in this text.

Political scientists often strive to develop a methodological rigor for research. Despite differences in methods, values, and theoretical influences, it is the aim of all political scientists to formulate ideas, test theories, and discover results based on systematic study and inquiry. The approach of this text is not different. The authors set out to show that there are consistent foreign policy themes and ideas that transcend American presidential administrations. These themes, expressed through the rhetoric of presidential doctrines, are representative of American foreign policy actions and behavior. Through the examination of five different presidential doctrines – those of Woodrow Wilson, Harry Truman, Richard Nixon, Jimmy Carter, and Ronald Reagan – and the National Security Strategy (2002) of George W. Bush, we hope to highlight both the connections that link presidential doctrines and American foreign policy rhetoric over the past century and note the differences resulting from the targeted threat, political ideology, president's world view, and the international environment.

Chapter 1

ON THE HISTORY AND USE OF PRESIDENTIAL DOCTRINES

Robert P. Watson

PRESIDENTS AND NATIONAL SECURITY

Presidential actions on behalf of national security and the use of military force have a long history, dating to the founding of the nation. The president's powers in the areas of national defense and foreign policy have expanded significantly since the Founding, to the extent that they would scarcely be recognizable to George Washington. However, they are nonetheless rooted in the Framer's vision for the office and the Constitution. The Constitution empowers the president to act on behalf of national security in a variety of ways. So too has the office evolved to provide presidents with a number of extra-constitutional tools by which to shape national security policy.

The Framers desired and designed a role for the president in national defense and foreign policy, most notably that of commander-in-chief, whereby the president was given discretion to *respond* to national emergencies and military attacks as well as to end any hostilities. The president's power to *initiate* offensive acts, however, was checked by assigning Congress the power to declare war ("war powers"). Suffice it to say, the arrangement that has evolved favors a leading role by the president. Whether rightly or wrongly, Congress is hardly an equal partner to the president when it comes to national security today.

Presidents have conducted hundreds of military actions over the country's history (see Appendix D) without a resolution of war from the Congress. For instance, war was not declared in Korea (Truman), Vietnam (L.B. Johnson, Nixon), Grenada (Reagan), Panama or the Persian Gulf (G.H.W. Bush), Bosnia or Kosovo (Clinton), or Afghanistan or Iraq (G.W. Bush). In fact, Congress has declared war only five times in American history, as is indicated in Table 1.1 (see also Appendix C).

Table 1.1. U.S. Declared Wars

- War of 1812
- Mexican War of 1846
- Spanish-American War of 1898
- World War I
- World War II

Additional powers such as the making of *treaties* was also divided between the president and Senate, acting in their capacity as an advisory and consenting body. Article II, Section 2 of the Constitution empowers the president to forge treaties, which are then subject to Senate ratification by at least a two-thirds vote. The particular dynamic of the treaty process varies, is influenced by the state of presidential-senatorial relations, and evolved to a degree by custom. For example, when George Washington first went to the Senate in August of 1789 to request its advice on and approval of a treaty with Native Americans in Georgia, what he encountered was a lengthy, quarrelsome debate. Before the debate concluded, Washington, accustomed to more respectful treatment and expecting immediate action, stormed from the chamber vowing never to return. He did not. Nor did subsequent presidents. Presidents adopted the practice of seeking advice from senators in private, but not before the body proper; although, treaties must still be formally approved by the Senate. Historically, the far majority of treaties introduced have been ratified without change, and those encountering opposition in the Senate tend to be withdrawn by presidents without a vote. Once again, there is a prominent role for the president in national security and foreign policy making, which can be traced to the Constitution and which has evolved to favor presidential leadership.

Presidents also have the power to formulate *international executive agreements*, although this mechanism evolved in somewhat of an extra-constitutional manner, as a result of presidents wanting to avoid the formal treaty ratification process. Executive agreements do not need formal congressional approval, although by custom presidents are expected to inform Congress of such actions. For instance, when Lyndon B. Johnson and Richard Nixon entered into such agreements covertly with South Vietnam (and other countries) Congress enacted legislation requiring the Secretary of State to submit all agreements to Congress within sixty days. When Nixon B and later Gerald Ford B failed to comply with this 1972 law by having agencies conduct their own agreements, Congress again acted. This time they mandated in 1977 that all U.S. agencies must also disclose agreements within twenty days of the action.

Agreements are informal arrangements between or among the United States and foreign governments that do not supercede any statutory or legislative action. If they touch upon legislative business they might be subject to a simple, bicameral majority vote. Nonetheless, presidents have creatively found ample room in which to utilize agreements. Not surprisingly, the volume of executive agreements has increased dramatically in recent years, becoming a viable tool for presidents to conduct national security and foreign policy.

Presidents have a host of other mechanisms and powers at their disposal. For instance, they can recognize countries, which Harry S. Truman did in 1948 with Israel and Jimmy Carter did in 1979 in the case of the People's Republic of China. Presidents can cut formal ties with foreign regimes, recall ambassadors, and act in other symbolic but important ways that influence national security and foreign policy. If a president extends "most favored nation" or "fast-track" status to a trading partner, declares a nation to be a supporter of terrorism, or enforces economic sanctions or embargoes, the results are not without consequence. Presidents can also appoint ambassadors and envoys, receive visiting heads of state, and command media attention, all of which shape U.S. national security and foreign policy. Indeed, in his capacity as commander-in-chief and chief diplomat, the president is the chief architect of U.S. national security and foreign policy.

WAGING WAR AND PRESIDENTIAL DOCTRINES

History of U.S. National Security

The threat and use of military force has been a staple of U.S. national security policy and a card played by presidents since Thomas Jefferson sent marines to liberate the crew of the ship *Philadelphia* and deal with pirates off Tripoli and a small force of American soldiers conducted a mission in Mexico in 1806. Such presidential actions were formalized as policy when James Monroe decreed in

1823 that U.S. influence extended throughout the western hemisphere and James K. Polk declared war against Mexico in 1846, and thereby greatly expanded American influence westward (Mexico relinquished claims to territory that would eventually become Arizona, California, New Mexico, Texas, Utah, and other states in the West).

The president is commander-in-chief and is charged with protecting the security of the nation through war or other means. Presidents of the early nineteenth century used military force only rarely to protect U.S. interests, and it was typically used internally to suppress the indigenous population for much of the country's history. However, precedents for the national security doctrines of modern times can be traced to the early 1800s when the Navy and Marines were dispatched to the Barbary Coast, Fijian Islands, and Samoa to protect U.S. shipping and trade. The rationale for military excursions in the name of national security expanded with time, as presidents used force to attempt to stabilize Latin America, exert U.S. influence over the hemisphere, promote U.S. interests in such countries as Nicaragua and Mexico, and defeat revolts in Chile, Colombia, China, Cuba. Each of these actions occurred before the start of the twentieth century, and they all have factored into contemporary notions of national security.

Through the first half of the twentieth century, U.S. intervention was widespread in Haiti, Colombia, the Dominican Republic, Nicaragua, and elsewhere. At the outset of the new century, the United States emerged as the dominant power in the hemisphere and as an empire with territories as far flung as the Canal Zone in Panama and the Philippines. Events in the latter half of the twentieth century such as the Cuban Missile Crisis, Vietnam War, conflict in the Middle East, and humanitarian intervention in Bosnia, Kosovo, Haiti, Rwanda, and Somalia both further shaped and reflected American national security policy. The successful end of the Second World War in 1945 positioned the United States as a *world* super-power. In the post-war era, the United States was one of two powers in what would emerge as the bipolar world of the Cold War. When the Soviet Union collapsed in 1989, the United States remained as the world's political, economic, and military power.

Presidential Doctrines

The enhanced status of the United States in world events resulted in the increase in power of presidents in international affairs. Two of the early turning points which put the United States and U.S. presidents on this path, were the Monroe Doctrine and the Roosevelt Corollary. These also mark two of the earliest presidential doctrines on national security. The presidency of James Monroe (1817-1825) is noted for the bold proposition that the United States opposed permanent colonization in the western hemisphere by European powers. Although lacking the means to enforce his swagger, Monroe expanded the nation's focus beyond its own borders. President Theodore Roosevelt (1901-1909), in his Corollary to the Monroe Doctrine, expanded on the initial proposition insofar as the United States would act to protect its citizens, property, and interests in the hemisphere, enforcing its supremacy in the region. Through TR's intervention in the Colombian-Panamanian conflict, construction of the Panama Canal, establishment of a powerful navy, and willingness to engage in international diplomacy (e.g., the Russo-Japanese War), the United States asserted itself on the world stage and presidents gained enhanced status (and powers) as key actors in both U.S. national security and international affairs.

The circumstances surrounding national security issues and the times have changed, but presidents have continued to play the key role in forging U.S. national security policy. Events such as the erosion of the British colonial system and the empires of old Europe, World War II, the rise of the Soviet Union and the bipolar system of the Cold War, the advent of nuclear weapons, and international terrorism have influenced the crafting of national security doctrines and furthered their importance in international affairs.

Presidents approach the task of protecting U.S. national security from a variety of perspectives. These collective actions are deemed *doctrines*, which are general and overarching strategies and objectives that define a president's approach to national security and typically carry the name of the president. A variety of theories and perspectives seek to explain presidential decisions regarding doctrines on national security and the use of military force. There are both domestic and international considerations that underlie presidential doctrines and, as is evident in the subsequent chapters in this book, presidents throughout the twentieth century faced different problems and sought to address these problems through different doctrines.

Rational choice theories assume that an individual (the president in this case) acts according to self-interest, given his or her knowledge of the facts and alternatives. Through such a lens, national security doctrines would reflect the best interests of the United States (and where suitable its allies). Such reasoning is often used in an attempt to understand national security doctrines. *Expected utility* theories suggest that an individual (the president) will act in a way that maximizes utility based on the probability of a certain outcome occurring. Still other analysts seek to understand national security doctrines by studying *presidential psychology* (personality and character).[8] What is clear is that no single model or theory fully explains national security doctrines or presidential decisions regarding national security. A host of actors and agencies B an entire national security bureaucracy now exists B both domestic and international, also exert influence on national security policymaking and presidential doctrines.

"Just" Doctrines

One common trait among presidential doctrines, national security policymaking, and the use of military force in the twentieth century has been the interest in the moral justness of U.S. actions. Whether in the form of humanitarian intervention or labeling a foreign threat "evil," presidential doctrines have sought (for political purposes and otherwise) to justify the morality of U.S. national security as the high ground of a "just war."

The *Just War Doctrine* itself is a rule-based, deontological doctrine assuming that justice occurs if certain rules are followed. There are two basic categories of norms to a "just" war: *jus ad bellum*, which is the justness of the cause of resorting to war to begin with; and *jus in bello*, or the justness of the means or conduct of war once it is under way. Patrick Hayden[9] and B. Orend[10] suggest that a third type of justness of war exists in *jus post bellum*, or the justice of the ending of hostilities and the transition from war to peace, which is pertinent to President George W. Bush's doctrine and military campaigns against Afghanistan and Iraq. The initial category B *jus ad bellum* B is generally perceived as existing prior (both chronologically and in terms of importance) to *jus in bello*, which places the contemplation of war before or above the actual conduct of war. This theoretically assures the first imperative is satisfied before the second is undertaken.

There are several tenets or principles of *jus ad bellum* that must be satisfied in order for a war to be just; and much attention is given to this priority in presidential doctrines. These are listed in Table 1.2. Similarly, once war has commenced, there are two principles to be met in order for the conduct of the war B *jus in bello* B to be just.[11] These are also listed below.

---

[8] For a discussion of various rationales for national security, see Barry Blechman and Stephen Kaplan, *Force Without War* (Washington, D.C.: Brookings Institution, 1978).

[9] Patrick Hayden, AThe War on Terror and the Just Use of Military Force,@ in Patrick Hayden, Tom Lansford, and Robert P. Watson, eds., *America=s War on Terror* (Hampshire, England: Ashgate Publishing, 2003).

[10] B. Orend, AJustice After War,@ *Ethics and International Affairs*, 16 (2002): 43-56.

[11] For a further discussion, see D. Lackey, *The Ethics of War and Peace* (Englewood Cliffs, NJ: Prentice Hall, 1989).

There is a fair amount of agreement on these concepts of a just war. For example, the UN charter discourages states from using war for political reasons such as the expansion of territory, and speaks to the justness of war only when it is conducted in self-defense. Likewise, several Hague Conventions, Geneva Conventions, and other important international conventions throughout the twentieth century B and particularly those after WWII B have clearly articulated the notions B such as protecting innocents from being military targets during war B embedded in the *jus ad bellum* and *jus in bello* notions of a just war. Presidential doctrines and national security policies have sought to establish the justness of U.S. policy and adhere to such principles. Presidential doctrines typically state quite clearly that U.S. policy is based on just foundations and adheres to universally accepted principles of a just war, as embodied in the language of UN documents. A possible exception to this would be George W. Bush's advocacy of "pre-emptive strikes." Of course, whether or not these principles are attained or can be attained, and whether presidential doctrines and national security policy satisfy such principles are subject to debate. These principles offer another instrument for assessing presidential doctrines and U.S. national security policy, and is used in this book.

Table 1.2. Principles for a Just War

Jus ad bellum
- right authority/legitimate authority: only the highest authority in the country has the right to declare war
- right intention/just cause: states must go to war only for the purpose of restoring peace or justice, or for self-defense or the defense of allies who are unjustly attacked, rather than for conquest, revenge, economic or political gain, and so on
- last resort: war is declared only after all other measures and means have been tried and exhausted
- likelihood of success: states must have a reasonable chance for success in order to commit to war, because if the odds for victory are low then the state cannot justify war and should pursue another remedy

Jus in bello
- proportionality: those going to war must consider the good with the bad, comparing for instance the ability to restore peace against the resulting cost of death
- discrimination: the effort to avoid non-combatant casualties by attacking only soldiers and military targets of the opponent must be followed

Presidential Regimes

Noted presidential scholar, Stephen Skowronek, offers a model of presidential policy regimes applicable to the study of both domestic and foreign policy, as well as national security.[12] *Regimes* are established as a result of conflict and an inability of the existing arrangement to resolve the matter, and become powerful and lasting arrangements for approaching policy issues. The structure of these presidential regimes is not entirely dependent on any single factor. Rather, the regime is defined by regime structure, views of the existing and proper political order, and policy organizing principles. Also apparent with each new presidential regime is an increase in presidential power, be it over domestic, national security, or foreign policy. However, unlike the domestic sphere, where a new presidential regime has marginal commitment from successive presidents of the other party, a distinctive trait of presidential foreign policy and national security regimes is that successive presidents of both parties demonstrate commitment (at least to some degree) to the structure, institutions, and practices of the transformative regime.

Regimes are neither entirely defined nor restricted by the Constitution. Even though a variety of perspectives exist on how to interpret the Constitution, in general three major perspectives and periods of constitutional interpretation pertaining to the presidency have occurred. These can be seen as: the Founding (Washington); the Civil War/Reconstruction (Lincoln/Grant); and New Deal (FDR). For the purpose of this book, it is safe to conclude that presidential "national security policy regimes" exist within these interpretations but are not bound by them.

According to Skowronek's model, several presidents have transformed policy on the domestic front to the extent that they have established regimes. These transformational regimes put in place structures and organizing principles that influenced policy for years, and produced a major rethinking – or at least an adaptation – of dominant views of the state of national security. Adapting Skowronek's work to the focus of this book, it would appear that six presidents can be credited with initiating domestic policy regimes. They are listed, in order, in Table 1.3.

---

[12] It should be noted that Bush, like three of his four predecessors, came directly to the presidency from the governor=s office, and thus had less direct foreign policy experience than many presidents. Yet, even though the same allegations were leveled at Jimmy Carter, Ronald Reagan, and Bill Clinton during their presidential campaigns and through the initial months of their administrations, all three exhibited more interest in both international affairs and a commitment to existing collective security arrangements.

Table 1.3. Presidents Who Transformed Domestic Policy

- Thomas Jefferson
- Andrew Jackson
- Abraham Lincoln
- Theodore Roosevelt
- Franklin D. Roosevelt
- Ronald Reagan

Each of these administrations addressed conflict by initiating new structures, organizing principles, and policy priorities that remained in effect (in a relative state of equilibrium) until the next transformative regime. Borrowing again from Skowronek's model, it is possible to adapt this model to national security policy. As such, there are fundamentally two distinct and dominant national security policy regimes that have existed in the United States. These are the McKinley/TR regime and the FDR/Truman regime. However, it is worth considering whether two earlier models, both predating these regimes and establishing U.S. national security and foreign policy on the international stage, are worth noting. The first is the Washington "quasi-regime" of American neutrality and isolationism; the second is the Monroe/Polk "quasi-regime" which expanded U.S. influence south and west in an initial international foray. Whether these can be classified as regimes is uncertain. Subsequent presidents did not necessarily adhere to their tenets, but both did have a relatively continuous, lasting effect.

The United States played little role in international affairs until late in the nineteenth century, and national security previous to McKinley and Theodore Roosevelt could be said to have been an amalgamation of views that included isolationism, manifest destiny, Indian removal, and westward expansion. Rather, both these early "quasi-regimes" provide an initial foray into systematic thinking about national security and implementation of broad doctrine. They were used only minimally and intermittently by subsequent presidents (Washington's neutrality and isolationism having more impact), most of whom generally lacked consistent policy on national security and international affairs. However, their influence was felt over the course of the nineteenth century and provided a rudimentary foundation for subsequent actions. These regimes are listed in Table 1.4.

Table 1.4. National Security Regimes

?	Washington (1789-1797)
?	Monroe/Polk (1817-1825/1845-1849)
•	McKinley/TR (1897-1909)
•	FDR/Truman (1940-1953)
?	George W. Bush (2001-)

Note: • = regime
? = possible of "quasi" regime

National Security Regimes

The Monroe/Polk Aquasi-regime@ was marked by rhetorical and symbolic engagement internationally and some policy engagement in hemispheric affairs. This is the start of a presidential foreign policy (and possible national security) regime and can be traced to such seminal actions as the Monroe Doctrine and the Mexican-American War. The McKinley/TR regime was marked by limited international engagement and economic expansionism around the world. This regime's influence can be seen in the Spanish-American War, U.S. colonial possessions, building of the Panama Canal, and TR's use of the "Great White Fleet" and involvement in international diplomacy (e.g., Russo-Japanese War). In terms of national security, these two initial regimes sought to safeguard the United States and the hemisphere from European aggression and expansion, while expanding American territory and influence. The FDR/Truman regime is marked by international leadership economically, politically, and militarily and the rise of collective security institutions and structures. WWII and the threat of the Soviet Union produced the CIA, National Security Council, a unified Department of Defense, the Marshall Plan, food aid program, containment, NATO, the United Nations, and numerous other structural, organizational, and policy responses that guided the post-War order until at least 2001.

As was mentioned above, unlike presidential domestic policy regimes, these "national security regimes" are followed by successive administrations of both parties. They also resulted in an increased role for the United States in international affairs and an increase in presidential power. In presidential national security regimes B as in the crafting and conduct of foreign policy and national security policy B presidents are given more discretion from Congress and the American public than they are in domestic policy. This notion has been suggested in Wildavsky's famous "Two Presidencies Thesis",[13] and it would thus appear that presidents have more leeway in forging national security regimes, and the effect of such regimes is greater and more lasting, than in domestic policy.

Additionally, all regimes demonstrated a willingness to use U.S. force beyond American soil and shared some fundamental organizing beliefs. Emily Rosenberg[14] offers a list of these common principles

- The belief that other nations should follow the American developmental experience;
- Faith in free markets and private enterprise;
- The benefits of free trade and international investment;
- Sharing information and culture internationally;
- Some role for government exists in regulating the aforementioned tenets and promoting U.S. trade and values internationally.

Of course, the presidential national security regimes differed in the degree to which these tenets were practices, and the first two "quasi-regimes" existed in an era defined by pre-industrial society, thus limiting the influence of internationalism. Rosenberg's list offers another means that will be used to examine the national security regimes and doctrines presented in this book.

The Post-WWII/Cold War Order

The organizing principles, structures and institutions, and beliefs of the FDR/Truman regime have governed the conduct of U.S. national security policy for a half-century. There have been variations in practice, but these have been more variations in *degree*, than variations in *kind*. One such occurrence was the Vietnam War, which was a new experience for the United States in that it was an unconventional, unpopular war that was not won. The FDR/Truman regime was tweaked by Richard Nixon during the Vietnam crisis. The Nixon doctrine advocated military and economic assistance to nations allied with the United States in the Cold War or if those state's freedoms or peace were threatened by an

---

[13] Neal Allen, AThe Fight Against Terrorism in Historical Context,@ in Patrick Hayden, Tom Lansford, and Robert P. Watson, eds., *America=s War on Terror* (England: Ashgate Publishers, 2003).
[14] Stephen Skowronek, *The Politics Presidents Make: Leadership from John Adams to Bill Clinton* (Cambridge, Mass.: Belknap Press of Harvard University, 1997).

enemy of the United States. The response was aid to Israel and Vietnam. Nixon offered three principles to govern how U.S. military force would be used:

- The U.S. would honor all treaties in responding to the invasion of allied lands;
- The U.S. would provide a nuclear umbrella for the world against other nuclear threats;
- The U.S. would provide military assistance but not commit troops in local conflicts.

Key presidential aides – typically secretaries of defense or state – have also advocated national security doctrines. One such – and another consideration for the conduct of war and national security – was offered by Caspar Weinberger, Secretary of Defense for President Reagan, who espoused a doctrine based on the experiences of Vietnam that was more cautious in its definition of U.S. national security interest and potentially limiting. A few years after Weinberger, Colin Powell would forward a similar doctrine for national security and warfare. Powell, George H.W. Bush's National Security Advisor and George W. Bush's Secretary of State, emphasized the following:

- Lining up support internationally and domestically before going to war;
- Having a narrow and clearly defined mission;
- Having a narrow and clearly defined ending point or exit strategy before proceeding with use of force;
- Using force as a last resort;
- If the decision is to use force, then so much power must be assembled that the outcome of the conflict is not in jeopardy.

An opposing doctrine to Weinberger (and possibly Powell) was offered by Reagan's Secretary of State, George Shultz, who attempted to tie humanitarian crises to U.S. national security. Shultz felt that the United States had a moral duty to use force under certain circumstances, and that such a use would inherently be just. A comparison of the Weinberger and Shultz doctrines is offered in Table 1.5, and points to the variations and different views on the subject even in the same administration.

Table 1.5. Weinberger v. Shultz Doctrines

Weinberger Doctrine
- war must be vital to U.S. national interests;
- if troops are used, the U.S. must be committed to victory;
- there must be clearly defined political and military objectives;
- the relationship between objectives and the situation of the war must be continually assessed;
- before going to war, one must be assured the American people and Congress support actions;
- force must be the last resort.

Shultz Doctrine
Force/war is justified when:
- aggression is attacking human freedom;
- aggression is imposing a regime against the will of the people;
- a regime is acting without regard for innocent life or the sanctity of life.

George W. Bush embarked on nothing short of establishing another presidential national security policy regime as seen to a degree before 9/11 and most explicitly since 9/11.

Bush's presidency is, like those of previous presidents identified with national security policy regimes, a transformational presidency. Like other transformational presidencies, Bush's policies are enhancing presidential power over the conduct of national security policy, establishing new institutional arrangements, and creating a new set of policy priorities and directions. Regimes are noteworthy for resulting in a rather stable equilibrium until the next transformative regime and, although at the time of this writing it is far too early to make any conclusions about such a lasting impact of the Bush doctrine, it would appear to have the potential to fundamentally change U.S. national security policy and international notions of collective security.

THE SIGNIFICANCE OF THE BUSH DOCTRINE

A New Doctrine, A New Regime?

George W. Bush came into office in 2001 with a different set of foreign policy and national security priorities than his two immediate predecessors. Bush made it clear during the 2000 presidential campaign that his administration would make less of a commitment to the existing institutions and mechanisms of collective security than perhaps any president serving since Franklin D. Roosevelt or even Woodrow Wilson, and less adherence to, and interest in, the genesis of collective security. Bush also demonstrated less interest in B and it is fairly safe to suggest that he had less of a grasp of B international affairs than any of his recent predecessors, and even possibly dating to Warren G. Harding.[15] Moreover, he faced a world order different from that of any of his predecessors except Bill Clinton, namely, the end of the Cold War and the international security and foreign policy organizing principles necessitated by it.

The first few months of the Bush administration produced a unilateral withdrawal of the United States from several high-profile international treaties and agreements, much to the consternation of U.S. allies in Europe as well as internationalists and multilateralists from both the Democratic Party and, to a lesser degree, the Republican Party. This was followed by the pronouncement by the Bush administration of a new set of national security and international priorities and commitments after the terrorist attacks of 11 September 2001 that signaled the potential of changing the focus and practice of American national security and foreign policy. Indeed, the initial years of the Bush presidency placed American national security policy at a crossroads, as we appear to be witnessing a change in approach more dramatic than at any point since the presidencies of FDR and Harry Truman.

What is emerging at the time of this writing is a Bush Doctrine that, depending on one's perspective, is either moving beyond or threatening to undermine the principles and practices of collective security initiated by those two aforementioned presidents, principles that have stood as the pillars of American (and European) security and foreign policy since the conclusion of WWII. As Neal Allen observes, neither the monumental changes occurring as a result of the fall of the Soviet Union and the end of the Cold War, nor George H.W. Bush's "New World Order" or Bill Clinton's "Humanitarian Intervention" had such an impact on national security thinking and practice.[16]

---

[15] Aaron Wildavsky, AThe Two Presidencies,@ in A. Wildavsky, ed., *Perspectives on the Presidency* (Boston: Little, Brown, 1975).

[16] Emily Rosenberg, *Spreading the American Dream: American Economic and Cultural Expansion* (New York: Hill and Wang, 1982).

Bush's Anti-Terror Regime?

The national security policies (and foreign policies) of the Bush administration are markedly different from those of Bush's predecessors operating under the FDR/Truman regime in several notable ways. In the areas of national security and foreign policy, it is perhaps seen best by:

- A unilateral withdrawal by the United States from the Middle East peace process (2001-2002), Palestinian-Israeli conflict, Kyoto (global warming) and other international environmental safeguards, the Anti-Ballistic Missile Treaty, and other international treaties and agreements;
- Something between (depending on one's views) ignoring and flat out hostility toward multilateral and internationalist actions such as an array of UN-sponsored initiatives, opposition to the war against Iraq, and international efforts to use courts of justice;
- The lack of new alliances, international structures or organizations, or policy commitments internationally of any significance by the United States;
- Establishment of new domestic organizations (homeland security reorganization) and processes (military tribunals) for national security.

Bush's national security strategy as applied to the war on terror advocates the use of "pre-emptive strikes," regime change, and the use of force against regimes or states determined to be harboring, sponsoring, aiding, or abetting terrorists. This policy deemed it necessary to overthrow the Taliban regime in Afghanistan by military force because of the regime's ties to the al-Qaeda terror network and its leader Osama bin Laden, who was the perpetrator of the 9/11 terror attack against the United States. A military invasion of Iraq was authorized (over objections by the UN and some key European allies) on the grounds that regime change was just when the regime was deemed to be Aevil@ and a potential terrorist threat because of its potential to develop weapons of mass destruction. The war on terror as envisioned by Bush involves a long-term, comprehensive strategy fought with financial, intelligence, cultural/educational, and military actions. The war is being waged internationally, with the United States freezing terrorists' financial assets, gathering intelligence, and using force where necessary. And the war is being waged domestically, where new structures such as the Department of Homeland Security have been created and a host of immigration, coastal, transportation, and law enforcement functions and agencies have been reorganized.

Numerous facets of Bush's national security policies/doctrine and the war on terror would seem to fit the criteria for a new national security regime. The President's actions and those of several of his senior officials have bypassed several of the institutions and mechanisms established under the FDR/Truman regime, have been unilateral in tone and occasionally in practice, and have sought to establish new structures and organizing principles. Several of Bush's national security policies B classifying individuals as enemy combatants to be dealt with external to the civil justice system and expanded use of military tribunals and FBI powers B are highly controversial and likewise seem to be an effort to ignore existing systems and processes. The Bush doctrine is certainly grand in scope and far-reaching and the enemy B international terrorists, especially al-Qaeda and other radical Islamic groups B certainly constitute a direct challenge to American values and culture.

The national security threat and response has, as Neal Allen has observed, dominated the U.S. national security, foreign, and domestic policy landscape.[17] For instance, the problems in Colombia with illicit drug production and the existing policy response have changed. It is no longer about drug interdiction (a favorite and high-profile initiative of George W. Bush's own party), rather it is now an anti-terrorist issue. American concerns over Russia's heavy-handed aggression toward Chechnya has morphed into support for a Russian anti-terror campaign.

CONCLUSION

Like the FDR/Truman regime and Cold War, Bush's national security doctrine (the *National Security Strategy of the United States*, 2002) and the war on terror have the potential to redefine U.S. national security policy at home and worldwide. Like previous regimes, Bush's actions have expanded presidential power in national security, changed existing structures, and developed new organizing principles for the conduct of national security and foreign policy. Like other presidential national security doctrines, Bush's NSS espouses the President's world view, is shaped by the international environment, identifies the enemy and security threats to the United States, and justifies the proposed action.

Whether or not the Bush's Doctrine builds on previous presidential doctrines and is shaped by them, or whether it signals a new approach to national security remains to be seen. Whether it is justified or unjust, whether it is necessary or

---

[17] Allen, 2003.

problematic, the Bush doctrine has the potential to usher in a new national security regime.

Chapter 2

WOODROW WILSON:
A TRADITION OF INTERNATIONALISM
IN AMERICAN FOREIGN POLICY

Charles Gleek

INTRODUCTION

Woodrow Wilson's ideas have had a profound influence on the foreign policy of the United States. Henry Kissinger describes Wilsonian idealism as the drumbeat to which American foreign policy continues to march.[18] Wilson scholar Earl Latham depicts Wilson's ideas as standing, "for the best in the American liberal tradition."[19] Arthur Link, a leading Wilson biographer, contends that the values Wilson fought and stood for have transcended generations.[20] More than almost any other American president in the twentieth century, Woodrow Wilson's influence and legacy is studied and debated amongst historians and political scientists today.

The purpose of this chapter is to highlight the principles that Wilson conveyed in his Fourteen Points speech of 8 January 1918. It is the belief of this

---

[18] Henry Kissinger, *Diplomacy* (New York: Simon & Schuster, 1994), 30.
[19] Earl Latham, *The Philosophy and Policies of Woodrow Wilson* (Chicago: University of Chicago Press, 1958), xv.
[20] Arthur S. Link, "The Higher Realism of Woodrow Wilson," *Journal of Presbyterian History*, XLI (March 1963), 2.

author – and a concept receiving much attention by scholars – that there are themes that run through the history of American foreign policy; that these ideas have been expressed through presidential doctrines; and that these ideas manifest themselves in the formation of foreign policy. The goal of this work is to see whether the ideas expressed in Wilson's Fourteen Points have influenced and materialized in modern political discourse.

For this essay, the ideas that are identified in Wilson's Fourteen Points will be compared to the concepts conveyed in President George W. Bush's National Security Strategy. The Bush National Security Strategy (NSS) has been described as the, "most significant U.S. foreign policy statement since NSC 68."[21] The Brookings Institution has called the NSS Bush's, "vision of a distinctly American internationalism."[22] Based on these and similar evaluations, President Bush's NSS is certainly a worthy subject for inquiry and comparison with Wilsonianism.

This study is not necessarily unique in its scope or coverage. For instance, Henry Kissinger's seminal work, *Diplomacy*, offers detailed analysis of the traditions that guide American foreign policy. Tony Smith's 1994 book, *America's Mission*, documents the efforts made by American administrations in fostering democracy around the world during the twentieth century. Michael Mandelbaum's *Ideas That Conquered the World* describes how the events of 11 September 2001 revealed that notions of peace, democracy, and free markets have become the status quo for the globe. Writing in *Time* magazine, Michael Elliot describes Bush's presidency as having "embraced a muscular Wilsonianism."[23] Recently, historian Walter LaFeber examined the emerging "Bush Doctrine" as a manifestation of traditions in American foreign policy.[24] However, as with all social science, knowledge is accumulated through the repetition of study as well as the expansion of discourse; this chapter seeks to add to the current dialogue.

METHODOLOGY

This chapter is not designed to be quantitative in nature. There is no systematic use of various control variables in an effort to identify a single causal factor to explain policy decisions. This study neither compares similar types of documents, i.e. doctrine to doctrine or security strategy to security strategy, nor

---

[21] Max Boot, "Doctrine of the 'Big Enchilada'," *Washington Post* (14 October, 2002), A29.
[22] Ivo H. Daalder, James M. Lindsay, and James B. Steinberg. "The Bush National Security Strategy: An Evaluation," *Brookings Institution*, Policy Brief #109 (October 2002).
[23] Michael Elliot, "The Trouble with Saving the World," *Time* (30 December 2002 & 6 January 2003).
[24] Walter LaFeber, "The Bush Doctrine," *Diplomatic History* 26: 4 (Fall 2002).

does it reject a single causal explanation for an event. The goal is to highlight the similarities between two primary source documents: Wilson's Fourteen Points speech and Bush's National Security Strategy. These similarities will be determined through the examination of rhetoric in each of the documents; no comparison will be made between policies and institutions that developed as a result of these documents. This exclusive examination of the rhetoric allows for the clear comparison of ideas. In addition, the exclusion of the operational and policy proscriptions advocated by each president would be impossible. Not only were some of Wilson's ideas never fulfilled, such as the active participation of the United States in the League of Nations, but there has not been adequate time for all of the policies and programs outlined in the Bush NSS to have been implemented. A future comparative study along these lines would certainly be interesting and necessary.

Using interpretation and understanding as a guide, ideas and principles expressed in both primary sources will be compared. This method does not exclude other causal factors for the existence of similar ideas between the documents. What this method does allow for is an interpretive case to be made that ideas in American foreign policy transcend history, administration, world events, and time.

To support this premise, the ideas offered by scholars in the field of political science are cited. Bagby identifies nine trends, for example, which he terms "basic foreign policies," that the United States has supported over time.[25] Some of these trends, including "collective security" and "international trade" are used in the comparative analysis presented here. Rosati contends that American foreign policy has always been active, experiencing both continuity and change over its history.[26] This activity is expressed in the rise of American power, in military, economic, and political terms, and the deepening involvement by the United States in events in the international system. Rosati dispels the traditional myth of American isolationism, arguing instead that the tradition in United States foreign policy has been one of active diplomatic, economic, and military engagement throughout the world. Goldstein & Keohane state that ideas themselves help to explain events in foreign policy. Particularly in times of uncertainty or crises, such as war, ideas act as a guide to behavior or as roadmaps for ethical or moral

---

[25] Wesley M. Bagby, *America's International Relations Since World War One* (New York: Oxford University Press, 1999), 11-14.
[26] Jerel A. Rosati, *The Politics of United States Foreign Policy* (2nd Ed.) (Fort Worth, T.X.: Harcourt Brace College Publishers, 1999), 20.

actions.[27] If Goldstein and Keohane are correct, ideas that Wilson presented in 1918 might offer pathways of behavior and policy formation that would be useful to Bush in 2002. In short, ideas and concepts in a state's foreign policy tend to transcend administrations.

What follows is the comparative structure used to analyze the two primary sources. Table 2.1. consists of a number of variables, or concepts, that are to be examined. Manifestations of these concepts in each of the primary sources will be documented, examined, and compared against one another. These concepts were chosen for two reasons. First they are expressed in Wilson's speech, and thus provide the basis for comparison with the NSS. Second, these concepts are identified as contemporary areas of interest and importance in American foreign policy. When applicable, additional analysis and scholarship will support the claims made in this interpretation. The summation of this comparison will identify the ideas and principles that Wilson espoused in the Fourteen Points that are also exemplified in the NSS.

Sartori identifies the importance of defining concepts in comparative study.[28] In order to reduce the confusion surrounding conceptual definitions used in this comparative study and the ensuing chapters in the book, the following definitions will be used: *international environment*, the state or condition of relations between and among states; *role of the U.S. in the international system*, the manner in which the United States behaves in terms of its diplomatic, economical, and military posture; *use of force*, efforts undertaken by states in an attempt to compel others to take certain course of action or to cease action; *arms control*, treaties or agreements amongst states that restrict or prohibit the research, development, deployment, or delivery of certain types of weapons systems; *collective security*, concept behind the League of Nations, the United Nations, and NATO, defined as the agreement between states that aggression against one state is equal to aggression against all member states, and that said aggression should be defeated collectively; *international trade*, from the liberal-capitalist perspective, the general subject of markets, commerce, and investment between and amongst states and corporations; and *self determination*, the right of peoples living within a geographic territory to determine their own political, economic, social, and legal status within their territory.

Table 2.1. Comparing Wilson's Fourteen Points and Bush's NSS

---

[27] Judith Goldstein and Robert O. Keohane, *Ideas & Foreign Policy: Beliefs, Institutions and Political Change* (Ithica, N.Y.: Cornell University Press, 1993), 16.

[28] Giovanni Sartori, "Concept Misinformation in Comparative Politics," *The American Political Science Review*, 64:4 (1970), 1033-1053.

	Wilson: Fourteen Points	**Bush: NSS**
International Environment	U.S. involvement in World War I; systemic war fought primarily in Europe, as well as the Atlantic Ocean, and Mediterranean Sea.	U.S. engaged in the global 'War on Terror'; active military operations in Afghanistan, Georgia, the Philippines, and Iraq, along with preliminary activities in the Middle East and in North Africa
Role of the U.S. in the International Society	"The program of the world's peace, therefore, is our program"; the promotion of American/universal values: justice, liberty, and security	"Distinctly American internationalism"; broad and deep involvement in world affairs; a responsibility promote values
Use of Force	"For such arrangements and covenants, we are willing to fight and to continue to fight until they are achieved"; force to be used to achieve principles	"(to defend the U.S.) Make use of every tool in our arsenal- military power"; defend principles and interests through preemptive use of force
Arms Control	"(Arms) Reduced to the lowest point consistent with domestic safety"; self-imposed and through agreements	Not specifically mentioned; ambiguous
Collective Security	"A general association of nations...affording mutual guarantees of political independence and territorial integrity"; reliance on organizations of states to maintain the peace	"The U.S. in committed to lasting institutions like the UN, WTO, OAS, and NATO; maintain present collective security organizations, use additional ad hoc coalitions, and act unilaterally if necessary
International Trade	"The removal...of all economic barriers and the establishment of equality of trade conditions"; free trade is beneficial to all	"Ignite a New Era of Global Economic Growth Through Free Markets and Free Trade"; U.S. national security is increased through free trade
Self- Determination	"The right (of all peoples and nationalities) to live on equal terms of liberty and safety"; addresses specific geographies and peoples	"Actively work to bring the hope of democracy, development, free markets, and free trade to every corner of the world"; addresses developing nations but not issues in Russia or China

FOURTEEN POINTS

The onset of World War I marked the end of the social and political conditions of the nineteenth century. In European society, the gradual improvement of social conditions and the political economy were reversed as states took up arms against each other. The balance of power system that had stabilized Europe for nearly a century disintegrated during the summer of 1914. During the war, long-standing empires, such as the Austro-Hungarian and Ottoman, collapsed as a result of the conflict that was fought across continents and oceans. Emerging powers such as the United States, Russia (later, the Soviet Union), and Japan became more active in international affairs. In terms of the war itself, modernity entered the battlefield in the form of tanks, aircraft, and chemical weapons. Characterized as the "war to end all wars," World War I wrought a level of destruction and violence to both soldiers and citizens throughout the world heretofore unseen.

Wilson's Speech, Wilson's Vision

On 8 January 1918, President Woodrow Wilson spoke before a joint session of Congress to outline his ideas for a post-war international order. Combs and Combs suggests that the Fourteen Points were designed to end the practices that Wilson identified as the causes of war; among them barriers to free trade, the arms race, and colonialism.[29] Responding to the war in Europe, Wilson essentially saw a blatant attempt by the German state to subjugate the Russian people. Thus, Wilson's speech provided a rallying point for peace-loving nations to gather around in reshaping their future relations.[30] In the speech, Wilson outlined the principles, which he believed would help states avoid the bloodshed of a future plagued by systemic war.

The Fourteen Points can be divided into two categories; those that deal with specific issues and those that are general statements about the international system.[31] Regarding the specific concerns, points VI through XIII focus on the conditions of geographic regions adversely affected by the war. In all of these

---

[29] Jerald A. Combs and Arthur G. Combs. *The History of American Foreign Policy, 2nd Ed.* (New York: McGraw-Hill, 1997), 223.
[30] Arthur S. Link, *Wilson the Diplomatist* (Baltimore: Johns Hopkins University Press, 1957), 102.
[31] President Wilson's Fourteen Points speech, in its originally delivered form, comes from: Arthur S. Link and William M. Leary, Jr. *The Diplomacy of World Power: The United States, 1889-1920* (New York: St. Martin's, 1970), 148-153. All references and quotations in this section refer to this citation.

areas, Wilson supports the idea of self-determination, or the ability for people to freely choose their own government. While there certainly has been some debate as to whether or not Wilson would have supported these states' right to form a communist government, the underlying theme Wilson presents is that colonial and repressive regimes are no longer legitimate forms of government.[32] As expressed in points IX and X, Wilson supports the right for people to form their own states, based on ethnographic lines.

It is important to reflect on the notion that Wilson addressed the problems of specific geographic and national areas – specifically, the right of Russia to preserve its territorial integrity and its right to "determine her own political development and national policy," the restoration of Belgium in order to preserve international law, the right of "other nationalities" under the rule of the Ottoman Empire to secure their own autonomous development. Wilson's focus was designed to bring about specific changes following the war. Without the enforcement of the idea of self-determination, the principles espoused in the Fourteen Points would become little more than empty rhetoric. This enforcement linked the principles that Wilson described as both American and universal to material improvements of the peoples of Europe.

Point XIV deals directly with the notion of collective security. Wilson advocated the establishment of an international organization, based on laws and covenants, with the express purpose of securing peace amongst states. Such an organization would work to eliminate aggression by providing a forum for the pacific settlement of disputes, deter aggression through collective responses to acts of war, and enhance cooperation by facilitating dialogue among member states. This point would ultimately lead to the establishment of the League of Nations, a precursor to the United Nations, where member states actively engaged in dialogue, cooperation, and diplomacy in an effort to maintain an environment of collective stability and security.

In regards to arms control, Wilson recognized that the gradual buildup of armaments amongst the European states had created an arms race. Expressed in point IV, Wilson advocates arms control in terms of, "Adequate guarantees and taken that national armaments will be reduced to the lowest point consistent with domestic safety." Implicitly, Wilson advocates both self-imposed regulations on arms, as well as binding treaties designed to secure (guarantee) that national armaments remain at a minimum.

---

[32] There are numerous books that deal with Wilson's personal views on Communism. Along with the previously cited works in this study, see especially: Thomas Knock, *To End All Wars*, 1992).

Wilson viewed international trade as a primary mechanism for non-violent interaction between states. As expressed in point III, the removal of economic barriers would establish, "an equality of trade conditions among all the nations consenting to the peace." Without protectionist tariffs, often established as tools for political advantage in domestic and international politics, Wilson's vision perceived a world where states would compete, not in the accumulation of arms, on the battlefield, or for colonial possession, but in the increase of wealth.

The Role of the United States

For Wilson, the role of the United States in the world was to promote peace and justice. "The program of the world's peace, therefore, is our program." In one single sentence, Wilson advocates that American ideas and values are universal, and that America has an interest in promoting and securing these interests around the world. Wilson also contends that the United States should use the mechanisms of international law, as well as cooperative means such as transnational trade and international organizations to achieve peace.

Wilson does not, however, reject the use of force outright. Referring to the Fourteen Points, he states,

> For such arrangements and covenants, we are willing to fight and to continue to fight until they are achieved; but only because we wish the right to prevail and desire a just and stable peace such as can be secured only by removing the chief provocations to war, which this program does remove.

Wilson's contention is that there are legitimate reasons for states to engage in war: to prevent the breakdown of international peace; to uphold international laws and norms; and in response to aggression. While Wilson's speech does provide mechanisms for legitimizing warfare and promoting conflict resolution through peaceful avenues, there is nothing in the Fourteen Points that explicitly prohibits a state from using force.

GEORGE W. BUSH'S NATIONAL SECURITY STRATEGY

There is little doubt that from the American perspective, the events of 11 September 2001 radically altered the American public's notions of global security and safety. In the 225 years of United States history, rarely has American soil been subjected to a successful, violent attack. The significance of 9/11 remains on the minds of most Americans even years after the tragedy. Numerous books and articles have been written on the subject of the changed international environment following 9/11. For the Bush administration, 9/11 brought the reality of a new security and ideological threat to the consciousness of the American people. No longer were the majority of Americans uninterested in world affairs. As seen in media coverage, on bookstore shelves, and across college campuses, Americans were suddenly very interested in world events. Within this context of public awareness for international affairs, the publication of the Bush NSS garnered significant public attention.[33]

Security in the Twenty-first Century

The NSS deals with a wide range of issues, far more than Wilson's Fourteen Points.[34] Reflecting on the "heritage and principles" of the United States, the NSS outlines the manner in which the United States will identify and address specific areas of security risk in the twenty-first century. Within the NSS, section titles range from "Champion Aspirations for Human Dignity" to "Work With Others to Diffuse Regional Conflicts" to "Transform America's National Security Institutions to Meet the Challenges and Opportunities of the Twenty-First Century." As most American presidents have done, either through rhetoric or policies, the NSS is a public presentation of American national interest.

The NSS frames the international environment in terms of a global terrorist threat, which is deemed "the gravest danger our Nation faces lies at the crossroads of radicalism and technology." Since the U.S.-led invasion of Afghanistan in October of 2001, the common term for this condition has been known as the "War on Terrorism." The United States has been actively engaged in military operations around he world, in an attempt to deter and prevent the spread of international terrorism.

The NSS explicitly supports the idea of self-determination. As outlined in the introduction, the NSS states that it is the intent of the United States to "create... conditions in which all nations and all societies can choose for themselves the rewards and challenges of political and economic liberty." In order to promote this liberty, the NSS outlines a guide for future United States behavior, including the use of foreign aid and bilateral relations.

---

[33] All U.S. Presidents are required by law, to publish a National Security Strategy of the United States as per the Goldwater-Nichols Department of Defense Reorganization Act of 1986.
[34] *The National Security Strategy of the United States*, The White House, September 2002. All references and quotations in this section refer to this citation.

Self-Interest and New Threats

At its outset, the NSS states that the United States will act in its own self-interest, and that this interest is similar to the interest of other states around the world. In terms of collective security, the NSS advocates developing regional and ad hoc coalitions of states to deal with emerging security threats. In addition, traditional security organizations such as NATO will continue to be relied upon, especially in its newly enlarged format and mission mandate. The NSS also recognizes that there is a possibility of a "renewal of old patterns of great power competition." With this in mind, the NSS advocates bilateral arrangements between emerging great powers such as Russia, China, and India.

A major theme of the National Security Strategy is that the current international environment is both radically different from the past and increasingly complex. Traditional threats from states have largely been replaced by threats from smaller, sub-state and non-state actors and terrorist organizations, and their potential use of weapons of mass destruction (nuclear, radiological, chemical, or biological weapons and delivery systems). In terms of arms control, the NSS expresses no singular view. On the one hand, the NSS implies arms control agreements, such as the recently abrogated 1972 ABM Treaty, are actually dangerous to the security of the United States, insofar as they restrict the ability of the United States to adequately defend against a missile attack. On the other hand, the United States will, "strengthen alliances," "work... to diffuse regional conflicts," and "prevent our enemies from threatening us, our allies, and our friends, with weapons of mass destruction." Such a strategy could imply a commitment to multilateral agreements regarding arms control.

"A strong world economy enhances our national security by advancing prosperity and freedom in the rest of the world." The subject of international trade occupies a large section of the Bush NSS. Reflecting liberal values and norms regarding tax policies, investment, and tariffs, the Bush NSS advocates increasing trade relations between states. The NSS suggests that such a trade scheme is not only important to the security of the United States, but is the best possible vehicle for developing nations to improve their own economies and societies.

In the complex and dangerous world described by the National Security Strategy, the role of the United States in the international system becomes increasingly diverse.

> "We will defend the peace by fighting terrorists and tyrants. We will preserve the peace by building good relations amongst the great powers. We will extend the peace by encouraging free and open societies on every continent."

This statement from the opening address of the NSS describes an America that will wear multiple hats around the globe. As arbiter, the United States will work to cooperate with other states on a wide range of issues. As crusader, the United States will engage "terrorists and tyrants" in order to secure peace. As defender, America ensure that the interests and allies of the United States are protected from the proliferation of weapons of mass destruction. As a leader, America will work to ensure that peoples around the world adopt the political, social, and economic values of the United States.

The use of force is explicitly advocated in the Bush NSS. "[to defeat threats] we must use every tool in our arsenal-military power, better homeland defenses, law enforcement, intelligence, and vigorous efforts." In addition, "We cannot defend America... by hoping for the best... the only path to peace and security is through action."

ANALYSIS

From this comparison, the following relationships can be determined and examined. First, there is some similarity in the international environment in which the Fourteen Points and the Bush NSS were drafted. Both Presidents issued their documents during times of war. In each case, there was a global consciousness and participation in warfare. The collapse of the European balance of power status quo during the First World War fundamentally altered the international environment during Wilson's terms in office. For the Bush administration, the new global security environment, conditioned in terms of being both post-Cold War and post-9/11 provides a similar context of change in the international system.

The solutions provided by both Wilson's speech and the Bush NSS convey similar themes. Bush identifies that the outcomes of the struggles of the twentieth century produced a "single sustainable model for success: freedom, democracy, and free enterprise." This model is a direct consequence of the points outlined by Wilson.

In terms of the issue of self-determination, there is both similarity and incongruence. On the surface, statements made about the rights of peoples to pursue their own governments are present in both documents. The major difference lies in the specificity of the statements. Wilson addressed all nations, particularly the great powers of the United Kingdom, France and Germany, in his calls to end the practice of colonialism. The Bush NSS addresses issues in primarily developing portions of the world. Important issues and regions are addressed in the NSS, as in Wilson's Fourteen Points, such as relations between Israel-Palestine and India-Pakistan, and the declining situation of the political economies of Latin America. There is no discussion, however, of the religious or ethnic persecution that occurs at the hands of Russia or China, powerful states that have had the most adversarial relationship with the United States in the last fifty years, despite the fact that the United States will, "speak out honestly about violations of the nonnegotiable demands from human dignity."

Regarding collective security, both documents recognize the need for cooperation with other states in promoting security issues. While the Fourteen Points places collective security in a paramount position, the NSS relegates it to secondary status and an *option* for American policy makers. In the NSS, there is no mention of the United Nations Security Council as a means for implementing collective security measures. The Fourteen Points stresses the need for mutual cooperation and enforcement of security guarantees amongst states, while the NSS views this path as simply one way of achieving security objectives. As with many of the concepts compared in this study, the NSS does not flatly oppose the principles expressed in the Fourteen Points. Rather, it offers modifications and options that did not or were not confronting or present in the United States in 1918.

Because of the ambiguity of the NSS regarding arms control agreements, there is little common ground to compare it with the Fourteen Points. Since this chapter does not deal with the application or material examples of the policies outlined in either document, it would be improper to extrapolate any further analysis on this subject.

Perhaps more than any other concept compared in this study, there is more common ground between the two documents regarding the notion of liberal international trade. While Wilson simply advocates the reduction of trade barriers and the complete freedom of the seas (significant issues in 1918), the Bush NSS delves deep into a strategy for promoting liberal capitalist norms around the globe. This similarity is not surprising, considering that the United States was itself founded on Adam Smith's ideas of free markets and commerce. Indeed, it would be shocking to find much deviation between any two presidents on this subject.

In both documents, interconnected visions of America's role in the international system are present. The Bush NSS states that, "we do not use our strength to press for unilateral advantage." Similarly, Wilson's Fourteen Points notes that, "What we demand in this war... is nothing peculiar for ourselves." Both documents suggest that the role for the United States is not to rise to a superior status above other nations, that the power America wields is not used in a hegemonic sense. Wilson's statement that, "this program of the world's peace, therefore, is our program" is echoed in the NSS, "this path (of peace, prosperity, and liberty) is not America's alone. It is open to all." As a result, the role of the United States in the international system can best be described in terms of global leadership and support, with varying degrees as to how to act in this capacity

Both documents advocate the use of force for maintaining American and global security. There are, certainly, degrees of difference between the two. Staying within the confines of his speech, Wilson advocated the use of force to fight for principles, rather than the use of force, as he saw it in 1918, used as a tool to perpetuate colonialism, poverty, and injustice.[35] The Bush NSS views the use of force as a viable means for state action in order to secure American national interest. This American national interest is linked with the interests of the rest of the world – in particular, freedom, democracy, and prosperity. For Wilson, the ends (justice and peace) regulate the means (use of force); for the Bush NSS, the ends justify the means.

There are a number of causal factors that would explain the differences between the Fourteen Points and the Bush National Security Strategy: The effects of history; the nature of the perceived threats to the United States; public awareness of international affairs; the relative power of the United States in terms of economy, political influence, and military capability – all of these concepts and many others could explain the differences between the two documents examined here. Perhaps one of the most important explanations could be seen in the efforts on the part of the Bush administration to show that they have a different theoretical perspective on world events than did previous administrations. While this essay does not seek to explore this avenue of inquiry, it would be inappropriate to avoid mentioning that the Bush Cabinet consists, almost exclusively, of persons who subscribe to the realist interpretation of international politics. For example, as exemplified in her 2000 *Foreign Affairs* article, Condoleezza Rice, who would become Bush's National Security Advisor, defines the national interest of the United States in realist terms.[36] Presumably as one of the primary architects of the Bush National Security Strategy, Rice's theoretical views on power, legitimacy, and the role of the United States are present in the NSS. It is interesting to note that in her article, Rice characterizes the previous Clinton administration as reflecting Wilsonian beliefs. Rice juxtaposes the Clinton administration against that of a future Republican administration, one that should

---

[35] A particularly interesting account of Wilson's administration and his views on the use of force can be found in Walter A. McDougall, *Promised Land, Crusader State*, 1997, Ch. 6.

[36] Condoleezza Rice, "Campaign 2000: Promoting the National Interest," *Foreign Affairs* (January/February 2000), 45-62.

act first in America's self-interest, and second in benefiting the larger community.[37] What this study indicates, despite Rice's article, is that there is the impression of Wilsonian ideas in the National Security Strategy.

A second explanation for the differences between the two documents lies in the complexity of the world in which they were written. It would be foolish to contend, given the manner in which modernity manifests itself in the twenty-first century, that the world of 1918 was more complex than the world of 2002. Whether by design, or because of other factors, the Fourteen Points address a limited number of issues. Theses are issues that Wilson felt, at the time, exacerbated the onset of war and threats to American national security. The Fourteen Points attempted to eliminate these threats through a variety of proscribed themes and actions. Similarly, the Bush NSS both addresses the threats to the United States and expresses the means for alleviating these threats. The Bush NSS advocates pathways to securing peace, both for the United States and the world at large. What is important to gather from this essay's analysis is that, despite the differences in the documentation, there are themes that Wilson articulated in his Fourteen Points speech – themes of free trade, self-determination, and a leadership role for the United States in the international system – that the Bush NSS expressly advocates as necessary for the security of the United States.

CONCLUSION

This study shows that there is some evidence that Wilsonian ideals are revealed in the Bush National Security Strategy. In reality, this is not surprising. All too often, especially in the public discourse surrounding American politics, references are made to various mores and themes that have existed in this country since its inception. Issues covered in the media, debated in Congress, and addressed by presidents are often framed in terms of American traditions. In foreign policy, this trend appears to be no different. There is some connection between the ideas Wilson expressed during the last year of World War I; ideas about commerce, the role that the United States should play in the world, the right for all peoples to determine their own form of government, that manifest themselves in Bush's National Security Strategy.

However, these are also material differences between the two documents. The NSS, despite the breadth of issues that it addresses, fails to reach the level of

---

[37] *Ibid.* p. 47.

specificity that the Fourteen Points did on certain issues, particularly in terms of self-determination. There are certainly differences between when and in what context force can be used, with the Bush NSS advocating, at the extreme, unilateral military action, something incompatible with Wilson's Fourteen Points. The notion of collective security, outlined rather simply in the Fourteen Points, has become a much more complicated endeavor; the Bush NSS reflects this complexity. Finally, the notion of arms control, specifically addressed by Wilson, finds little or no place in the Bush NSS.

It has been a tradition in American foreign policy to reflect on the past, and to perpetuate the ideas and visions previous administrations have put forth. To return to Kissinger, "By the beginning of the last decade of the twentieth century, Wilsonianism seemed triumphant."[38] The principles expressed in Wilson's Fourteen Points came to permeate American foreign policy ideas in the twentieth century. George W. Bush, as presented in the 2002 National Security Strategy, has continued this tradition into the twenty-first century. No doubt future administrations will continue to promote the ideals and values that have consistently defined and reflected the nation.

---

[38] Kissinger, *Diplomacy*, 804.

Chapter 3

HARRY S. TRUMAN AND THE LEGACY OF CONTAINMENT

Michael Grillo

INTRODUCTION

At the conclusion of World War II the United States emerged as a global superpower. With this enhanced status came a greater responsibility to the world. Prior to the war, America had been an inward looking nation. By the war's end the United States had abandoned its isolationism in exchange for the responsibilities of being a world leader. Harry S. Truman was the first president of this new era of American foreign policy, which also coincided with the beginning of the Cold War with the Soviet Union. In light of these circumstances, it has often been held that Truman had been given one of the worst presidential inheritances known to the office.

Conversely, George W. Bush's administration, the second to hold office since the end of the Cold War, had enjoyed an easy transition to the White House, as the United States had long been established as a global economic and military power. However, the events of 11 September 2001 had dramatically changed the face of world politics, as the United States and its allies now realized the threat of global terrorism. It is apparent that both Truman and Bush faced significantly different international threats and conditions during their presidencies. However, both presidents share striking similarities in their presidential doctrines, as they exhibit common trends of American foreign policy behavior that transcend both party affiliation and international conditions. Moreover, both presidential doctrines also advocate the employment of foreign economic aid as a tool for promoting American interests in the international arena, as well as containing enemy threats.

This chapter sets out to explore the similarities and differences between the Truman Doctrine and George W. Bush's *National Security Strategy*. Their similarities will be examined in the context of American foreign policy behavior and policy prescriptions, while their variances will be contrasted in terms of international environment and security threats.

HISTORICAL BACKGROUND

On 12 April 1945 Harry S. Truman entered the White House as the thirty-fifth president of the United States. As Franklin D. Roosevelt's successor, the new president had inherited World War Two, which Truman ended with the decision to use the world's first atomic weapons against Japan. After the Japanese surrender on 14 August 1945, Truman was now responsible for the transition to peacetime affairs, during which he hoped to continue Roosevelt's legacy in forging a mutual relationship with the Soviet Union. However, Roosevelt's dreams would never come to fruition.

The Grand Alliance

Within a year of Truman's presidency the "Grand Alliance" (among the U.S., Britain, and the Soviet Union) began to deteriorate. The need to defeat the Axis powers (Germany, Italy, Japan) was the primary reason for the Alliance's existence. After Japan had surrendered, the War was over. In the absence of a common security interest, the Grand Alliance disintegrated. Thus, the United States and the Soviet Union were once again enemies. The escalation of the Cold War during the Truman administration would force the United States to permanently abandon its prewar isolationism in exchange for a policy of containment, which sought to prevent the spread of communism in Europe and the Far East.

Historians have often debated the reasons for the Alliance's breakdown. Although Truman was not entirely to blame for the onset of the Cold War, he was partially responsible in the context of his limited knowledge of international relations, which made him more susceptible to the anti-Soviet views that were held by his advisers. On the other hand, the Soviet Union, under Joseph Stalin, pursued more aggressive policies of expansion after the war. In the face of Soviet expansionism, Truman had few options at his disposal. This would ultimately set the stage for the Cold War.[39]

Shortly after his entrance into the White House, Truman's advisers had begun to pressure the new president to take a more aggressive approach against the Soviet Union. Western European allies, especially British Prime Minister Winston Churchill, also supported these sentiments. On 16 April 1945, Truman and Churchill communicated their demand for the Soviet Union to stand by the Yalta Accord on Poland. Under this agreement, the Soviets would maintain control over Eastern Poland, while the Polish government would be given lands in the North and the West, as a reparation from Germany. The Soviets did not fulfill their part of the agreement, and in late April, Soviet Foreign Minister Vyacheslav Molotov was criticized by Truman at a White House meeting. By May 1945, the United States had ceased all foreign aid to the USSR, with the exception of support for the Soviet campaign against the Japanese. The Soviets had reacted harshly to its Western European and American allies by accusing the United States and Great Britain of attempting to shape Soviet policy towards Poland. In reaction to what it viewed as allied aggression, the Soviet government moved forward to establish communist regimes in Romania and Bulgaria.[40]

The United Nations organizational conference ended on 25 April 1945 in discord, as the result of disagreement between the Americans and Soviets. Truman's Secretary of War, Henry Stimson, had warned that the Grand Alliance must be sustained, as the Soviets were needed in the war against Japan, which was still in progress. Understanding the necessities of the war, Truman complied with his advisors. Shortly after, Truman had sent a diplomatic envoy to Moscow in order to reconcile differences with the Soviet government. The exchange was successful, and for a short period, tensions were eased. During the meeting, the Truman administration had accepted the Polish government, in which Stalin had allowed the participation of a handful of pro-Western Poles. In return, Stalin also accepted the 1947 Rio Pact, which instituted a regional alliance between the United States and its Latin American neighbors, thus establishing U.S. dominance in the Western Hemisphere. Stalin had also worked with the United States to finalize plans for the United Nations. The United Nations' charter was eventually

---

[39] Ronald E. Powaski, *Cold War: The United States and the Soviet Union, 1917-1991*, (New York: Oxford University Press, 1998), 65-67.
[40] Powaski, 67-68.

completed during the San Francisco Conference and was ratified on 25 June 1945.[41]

The Post-War Order

At Truman's invitation, Stalin joined him and Churchill at Potsdam, Germany in order to draft plans for the end of the war. The Allied leaders had decided to create a Council of Foreign Ministers, which would draft peace treaties for the defeated Axis powers, in addition to addressing the territorial issues that arose after the war. Moreover, the Allies had decided the future of Germany, which they believed must democratize, demilitarize, and de-Nazify; Nazi war criminals would be tried for crimes against humanity. The Potsdam Conference also established occupational zones for Allies in Germany, where each nation would extract reparations from its respective zone. However, it was agreed that the fate of Berlin would be decided at a later conference. The Soviets promised to invade Japanese held territories in Manchuria. Truman also alluded to the atomic bomb, which by this time had been successfully tested. Initially, the Truman administration had hoped that the use of the atomic bomb on Japan would force its unconditional surrender before the Soviets entered the war in August. However, this plan was not successful, as the Soviet Union declared war on Japan two days after the first atomic bomb had leveled Hiroshima.[42]

The breakdown of the alliance began at the London Conference of Foreign Ministers in September of 1945. The purpose of the conference was to discuss peace treaties. Both the United States and the Soviet Union had drafted their own respective versions of the treaties, as both had their own interests in mind. The Soviet Union, represented by Molotov, pressed the United States and Great Britain to accept their version of the Romanian and Bulgarian peace treaties in return for Soviet acceptance of the Anglo-American's Italian treaty. In addition, Molotov demanded that the Soviets be included in the postwar occupation of Japan. Secretary of State James Byrnes rejected the Soviet proposals, ending the conference in consternation. Shortly thereafter, the USSR attempted to compel Turkey to grant the Soviet navy full access to the Bosporus and Dardanelles straits. These straits were of strategic importance to the Soviet Union, as they

---

[41] Robert L. Messer, *The End of an Alliance: James F. Byrnes, Roosevelt, Truman, and the Origins of the Cold War*, (Chapel Hill: The University of North Carolina Press, 1982), 53-66.

[42] Paul Boyer, "Some Sort of Peace': President Truman, the American People, and the Atomic Bomb," *The Truman Presidency*, Edited by Michael J. Lacey, (New York: Cambridge University Press, 1991), 174-190.

linked the Black Sea to the Mediterranean. In the Middle East, the Soviets increased pressures on Iran in order to obtain greater access to Persian oil and other oil reserves.[43]

Although tensions were mounting, both the United States and the Soviet Union still attempted to forge a lasting peace. In December of 1945, Byrnes had traveled to Moscow and was able to ease tensions through a series of compromises concerning Romania and Bulgaria. Stalin had agreed to grant pro-western parties nominal representation within these communist governments. In return, the United States agreed to recognize the legitimacy of Romania and Bulgaria. Additionally, Byrnes and the Soviet foreign ministers decided to meet in Paris five months later in order to complete the unfinished peace treaties of the London Conference of Foreign Ministers. Furthermore, Byrnes consented to the establishment of an Allied Control Council that would advise General MacArthur on occupational measures for Japan. As Ronald E. Powaski notes, "As a result of these agreements, the Americans and the Soviets were able to fashion a face-saving way of recognizing their respective spheres of influence."[44]

Byrnes and the Soviets had also reached an agreement to establish a United Nations Atomic Energy Commission. However, Byrnes had overstepped his bounds, as he had ignored a previous agreement between Truman, Great Britain, and Canada, which called for nuclear disarmament measures and the sharing of nuclear energy with the Soviet Union. One of the primary stipulations of the agreement stated that these measures would not be implemented until an international inspection system was put into effect. Eventually, Byrnes was able to persuade the Soviets to accept this facet of the agreement. At the same time, he had lost a significant amount of credibility with hawks in Congress who believed that he was too soft with the Soviet Union. President Truman also agreed with the hardliners in Congress. As a result, James Byrnes submitted his resignation as Secretary of State in April of 1946 and would leave after the completion of the peace treaties later that year.[45]

Escalation and Decisions

Truman was pressured by anti-Soviet hardliners both at home and abroad. British foreign minister Ernest Bevin strongly advocated resistance to Soviet policies towards Iran and Turkey, as Great Britain was concerned with Soviet

---

[43] Powaski, 68.
[44] Ibid.
[45] Ibid, 68-69.

expansion into Western Europe, a threat which they would need U.S. support to curtail. The position of anti-Soviet hardliners was further solidified by the actions of the Soviet Union. On 9 February 1946, Joseph Stalin made an address to the Soviet people calling for a new five-year economic plan that would prepare the Soviet Union for a conflict with the West. This confrontation with the capitalist world, as Stalin noted, was inevitable. Furthermore, the Soviets had not yet withdrawn from Iran, as they had agreed to do, and continued to occupy Manchuria despite the surrender of Japan.

In early 1946, the media had reported that the Soviets had established a spy ring in the United States, which had successfully divulged top-secret information about America's nuclear weapons program. This resulted in an outcry that called for even harder policies against the Soviets, which included, above others, the maintenance of the U.S. monopoly on nuclear weapons. The Democratic administration also received a backlash from the Republican Party, who stated that they would no longer support Byrnes' policies towards the Soviets.[46]

Outside of the anti-Soviet rhetoric of the Republicans and Allied powers, the administration had already begun to implement more aggressive policies toward the USSR. On 12 February 1946 the State Department withdrew its recognition of the communist ruled Bulgarian government until it had reached an agreement on reparations with the Greek government. Ten days later, the United States had committed its support to Iran in promoting their independence and territorial integrity. The administration recognized the importance of Middle Eastern oil, especially that of Saudi Arabia, which it viewed as one of the greatest sources of material and geo-strategic power. Thus, the United States solidified its ties with Turkey, which was viewed as a gateway to the Middle East. In response to Soviet pressures on Turkey, Byrnes sent the nation's most powerful warship, the U.S.S. *Missouri*, to Istanbul in order to warn the Soviets against aggressive actions toward Turkey. Within a relatively short period, the Truman administration fashioned a new policy against the Soviets.

Containment

The logic behind this new policy was provided by the U.S. ambassador to Moscow, George Keenan. Totaling over 8,000 words, Keenan's long telegram

---

[46] Bruce R. Kuniholm, "U.S. Policy in the Near East: The Triumph's and Tribulations of the Truman Administration, *The Truman Administration*, Edited by Michael J. Lacey (New York: Cambridge University Press, 1991), 301-315.

provided the impetus for future U.S. policies towards the Soviet Union.[47] Keenan stated that the Soviet ideology was the basis for Joseph Stalin's worldview, which held that the western capitalist world was inexorably hostile. Thus, the swelling tension between the United States and the Soviet Union was not the result of a lack of communication or misunderstanding, but rather an axiom of the Soviet Marxist ideology. As George Keenan wrote:

> In this [communist] dogma, with its basic altruism of purpose, they found justification for their instinctive fear of the outside world, for the dictatorship for which they did not know how to rule, for the cruelties they did not dare not to inflict, for sacrifices they felt bound to demand. In the name of Marxism they sacrificed every single ethical value in their methods and tactics. Today they cannot dispense with it. It is fig leaf of their moral and intellectual respectability. Without it they would stand before history, at best, as only the last of that long succession of cruel and wasteful Russian rulers who have relentlessly forced [their] country on to ever new heights of military power in order to guarantee external security of their internally weak regimes…..[48]

Keenan ultimately held that the Soviet Union's aggressiveness was inherent in their ideology. He further noted that their enmity towards the capitalist system further legitimized Soviet totalitarianism and the oppression of their people. Keenan therefore believed that the ideological differences between the United States and the Soviet Union would not be reconciled by way of diplomacy. Thus Keenan prescribed that the United States should focus its efforts on containing the expansion of Soviet power. Keenan was not the only person in the administration to hold this point of view. Dean Acheson also believed that the Soviets could not be negotiated with, as he once stated, "You cannot sit down with them."[49] This new policy of containment would highlight the Truman administration's foreign policy toward the Soviets and would later provide the foundations for the Truman Doctrine.[50]

The policy of containment was fully accepted by Western European allies. Former British Prime Minister Winston Churchill once commented, "I am convinced that there is nothing they (the Soviets) admire so much as strength, and there is nothing for which they have less respect than for military weakness."[51]

---

[47] Powaski, 69-70.
[48] Henry Kissinger, *Diplomacy*, (New York: Simon and Schuster, 1994), 448.
[49] Arnold A. Offner, *Another Such Victory: President Truman and the Cold War, 1945-1953*, (California: Stanford University Press, 2002), 204.
[50] Kissinger, 446-450.
[51] Powaski, 70.

The first act of containment policy was the U.S. demand that the Soviets withdraw from Iran, as stated in a publicized note that Byrnes had sent to Moscow. The issue was later brought before the UN Security Council, at which time the Soviets decided to withdraw from Iran, with the promise of oil concessions, which the Iranians had cancelled once they gained independence. This initial test of containment policy proved to be successful. However, this event would mark the end of the Grand Alliance. Shortly thereafter, the Soviet Union rejected membership to the World Bank and the International Monetary Fund, declined a U.S. loan of $1 billion, and furthered its support for communist groups in China.[52]

By 1947, the issue of Greece had gained prominence in Cold War politics. Occupied by Great Britain at the end of the Second World War, Greece had been ravaged. Greece had become immensely unstable as a result of economic hardships coupled with the problems of reconstruction and relief. Furthermore, Greece was in a state of civil war, as the right-wing government of Constantine Tsaldares faced the internal threat of insurgent communist and socialist groups, while also coping with the external threat of belligerent neighbors within the Balkan region. The British in turn, had to deal with an economic crisis of their own and were ill equipped to manage the Greek crisis. As a result, in February of 1947 the British government alerted the United States that it could no longer shoulder the growing crisis in Greece. The Truman administration decided to assume responsibility for assisting the Greek government.[53] A number of people in the administration, most notably General George Marshall, were troubled by the British withdrawal, as it would also lead to a British withdrawal in the Middle East. As Saul Landau has noted, "As self assured heirs to the Pax Britannica, U.S. leaders viewed a communist victory in Greece the Greek civil war as unacceptable because such a victory would establish a trend away from capitalism in Europe." Strategically, Greece was seen by U.S. policymakers as a test of U.S. will and credibility among other Western European nations, and as a gateway for U.S. access to the great resources of the Middle East.[54]

THE TRUMAN DOCTRINE

On 12 March 1947, President Harry S. Truman addressed a joint session of Congress, declaring "that assistance to Greece is imperative if Greece is to survive

---

[52] Offner,180-184.
[53] Offner, 185-190.
[54] Saul Landau, The Dangerous Doctrine: National Security and U.S. Foreign Policy, (London: Westview Press, 1998), 37.

as a free nation."[55] President Truman requested that Congress approve $300 million to assist Greece against communist insurgency. Truman's speech emphasized the danger that Greece had faced. "The very existence of the Greek state is today threatened by the terrorist activities of several thousand armed men, led by Communists, who defy the government's authority at a number of points, particularly along the northern boundaries."[56] In addition, Truman also requested another $100 million to assist Turkey. Economic aid for Turkey was the result of the recognition that Turkey was "essential to the preservation of the Middle East,"[57] as the result of oil and its geo-strategic proximity to the Soviet Union.

The Truman Doctrine signaled a new American foreign policy. Many critics of Truman viewed this as an aggressive anti-Soviet policy that not only sought to contain communism, but to dictate the domestic politics of foreign nations, thus heralding American expansionism. Advocates of the Truman Doctrine believed that it was a necessary measure in promoting U.S. security. Truman argued that it was the responsibility of the United States to assist Greece, stating, "The free peoples of the world look to us for support in maintaining their freedoms."[58] Ultimately, the Truman Doctrine would lead to the creation of the Marshall Plan. Secretary of State George Marshall, who was Byrnes' successor, created the program. The Marshall Plan was a large-scale economic aid program that would assist war torn nations in Europe. Marshall believed that mending the economic and social destruction of the war would successfully deter domestic insurgency, as well as the external threat of Soviet communism. The Marshall plan would take the principles of the Truman Doctrine and apply them to Western Europe. By 1952, the United States had provided Western Europe with over $12 billion in economic aid. According to Harry S. Truman, the Truman Doctrine and the Marshall plan were "two halves of the same walnut."[59]

COMPARING PRESIDENTIAL DOCTRINES

The purpose of this examination is to compare and contrast Harry. S. Truman's Doctrine with George W. Bush's National Security Strategy (NSS). For the purposes of this analysis, the two presidential doctrines will be compared in terms of substantive rhetoric and recommended policy prescriptions. In terms of

---

[55] *The Truman Doctrine*, March 12, 1947.
[56] Ibid.
[57] Ibid.
[58] Ibid.
[59] Offner, 201-212.

the rhetoric employed by both doctrines, the similarities are remarkable, as both exhibit fundamental principles of American foreign policy behavior. In terms of policy prescriptions, only one similarity exists: economic aid. However, the use of economic aid by the Truman administration and all subsequent administrations, including that of George W. Bush, shows that it has become a prominent tool of American foreign policy. This comparison considers the practical application and effectiveness of these policies, as it is too early to weigh the success, or failure, of the foreign policy of the Bush administration.

In terms of contrasting the differences between the two doctrines, this analysis investigates the breadth and comprehensiveness of each presidential doctrine and its goals. These dissimilarities will be observed within the context of the international environments that produced them, as Harry S. Truman and George W. Bush are the products of two strikingly different eras of American foreign policy. Likewise, each administration faced challenges and circumstances that were inherently different.

It is evident that a number of similarities exist between the Truman Doctrine and George W. Bush's National Security Strategy. First, both presidential doctrines exhibit specific themes of American foreign policy, which embody the general ideological values of American political culture. The most notable among these themes are idealism and ethnocentrism. Second, both the NSS and the Truman Doctrine utilize economic aid as a means of securing American interests abroad, in addition to containing the influence of enemy forces.

Idealism is a pervasive element of American foreign policy behavior. The United States has always exhibited a "crusader mentality" in its approach to foreign relations. As Howard J. Wiarda notes, "Americans want their foreign policy to be moral, ethical, and idealistic."[60] The United States has a distinct set of ethics that places value on life and liberty without threat or oppression. Americans in turn, also look to instill these values in other nations, defending freedom, democracy, and human rights abroad. Truman himself stated these principles in his address before Congress. "One of the primary objectives of the foreign policy of the United States is the creation of conditions, in which we and other nations will be able to work out a way of life that is free from coercion."[61] Truman further noted, "I believe that it must be the policy of the United States to support free peoples who are resisting attempted subjugation by armed minorities or by outside pressures."[62]

---

[60] Howard J. Wiarda, *American Foreign Policy: Actors and Processes,* (New York: HarperCollins College Publishers, 1996) 41.
[61] *The Truman Doctrine.*
[62] Ibid.

Truman's views of American foreign policy completely lend themselves to the idea of the moral crusader who bears the responsibility of securing freedom and justice to those who are denied of it. This mentality is also evident in President Bush's National Security Strategy. In the second paragraph of the NSS Bush states,

> In keeping with our heritage and our principles, we do not use our strength to press for unilateral advantage. We seek instead to create a balance of power that favors human freedom: conditions in which all nations and all societies can choose for themselves the rewards and challenges of political and economic liberty.[63]

Sanctification and Ethnocentrism

Another facet of American idealism is its tendency towards sanctification, which renders conflict in terms of good versus evil. In the instance of Truman, the communist-led factions threatening Greece were demonized. In the case of George W. Bush, international terrorism is the evil element that threatens the world; as the NSS states, "The enemy is terrorism-premeditated, politically motivated violence perpetrated against innocents."[64] The rhetoric utilized by Truman and Bush is relatively analogous, as it embodies American idealism. Both doctrines live up to the notion that it is the moral responsibility of the United States to assist those who are denied life, liberty, and happiness, so that evil will not prevail.

Lending itself to idealism, ethnocentrism is also a decisive element of American foreign policy behavior. Although all societies are ethnocentric to certain degrees, Americans do have a superiority complex in that they feel that their ways are indeed the best. This is largely the product of the overall success of America, as it is among the wealthiest democracies in the world. In keeping with idealism, the United States prides itself on being the leader of the free world. As such, Americans look to export their institutions and principles to other nations. The Truman Doctrine proclaims, "If we falter in our leadership, we may endanger the peace of the world."[65] This statement is obviously rooted in the principle of U.S. leadership, in that Americans know what is best for the world and must serve as a guiding light to other nations.[66] The NSS states, "The United States must

---

[63] *The National Security Strategy of the United States of America,* September 2002.
[64] Ibid.
[65] *The Truman Doctrine.*
[66] Wiarda, 41.

defend liberty and justice because these principles are right and true for all people everywhere."[67]

These principles also apply to U.S. support of economic liberalism. "The lessons of history are clear: market economies, not command-and-control economies with the heavy hand of government, are the best way to promote prosperity and reduce poverty."[68] Once again, American idealism sets out to better the world by instilling its values and institutions abroad, as they have proven to be the formula for success in the United States.

The Use of Aid and Containment

When examining the policies of both the Truman and Bush administrations, it is clearly evident that each employ a variety of tactics to secure American interests in the international arena. Bush's NSS incorporates a large number of strategies, while the Truman Doctrine has only one. However, the use of economic aid is a significant device of American foreign policy, which has been utilized by all modern presidents from Franklin D. Roosevelt to George W. Bush. In the cases of Truman and Bush, both of their doctrines call for economic aid. Furthermore, both administrations employ economic aid as a way of curtailing and containing enemy influence. For the Truman administration, the enemy lay in the Soviet Union and the spread of communism. For George W. Bush, the enemy is terrorism and fundamentalist ideologies. Although the enemies are different, the remedy of economic prosperity is the same.

The Truman administration called for economic aid for Greece and Turkey. Although Turkey was included for geo-strategic purposes, Greece faced the threat of a total collapse to communist insurgents. The Truman administration had believed that if Greece fell to communism, there was the potential that the situation would diffuse. Thus, Truman addressed the issue to Congress. Secretary of State George Marshall believed that the best way to avoid such a potential threat in the future was to eradicate economic strife, which was viewed as the primary cause of Marxist insurgency. It was this belief that led to the establishment of the Marshall Plan, which was an extension of the Truman Doctrine. The Marshall Plan encouraged European nations to work together for economic recovery after WWII. The Marshall Plan began in April 1948, when Congress instituted the Economic Cooperation Administration to administer

---

[67] *The National Security Strategy of the United States of America.*
[68] Ibid.

foreign aid to Europe. From 1948 to 1952, the United States sent approximately $13 billion in food, machinery, and other products to Western Europe. Economic aid was also offered to the Soviet Union and its satellite states. However, the Soviet Union indignantly refused the offer, as it did not want to lose its sphere of influence in Eastern Europe.

Ultimately, the Truman Doctrine and the Marshall Plan were a success, in that they effectively contained the spread of communism to Western Europe. Economic aid and free trade allowed Western European nations to achieve peace and stability. Eastern Europe had already made the transition to communism prior to the Truman Doctrine. Out of fear of a Soviet backlash, Eastern Europe could not accept assistance from the United States. However, communism was confined to the Soviet sphere, as it did not spread to the nations that were assisted by Truman's foreign aid policies.

Although not implicitly stated, President Bush's National Security Strategy also works toward a policy of containment. Whereas the Truman administration aimed at containing communism, the NSS aims at the containment of terrorism and Islamic fundamentalism. However, the NSS, like the Truman Doctrine, recognizes that economic prosperity and democracy are decisive tools in preventing nations from falling into the hands of radical regimes, such as the Taliban in Afghanistan. The National Security Strategy explicitly emphasizes the importance of economic aid as a vehicle for promoting U.S. interests abroad. "We will use our foreign aid to promote freedom and support those who struggle non-violently for it, ensuring that nations moving toward democracy are rewarded for the steps they take."[69] In terms of containing terrorism, the Security Strategy states that the United States must, "support moderate and modern government, especially in the Muslim world, to ensure that the ideologies that promote terrorism do not find fertile ground in any nation."[70] This is comparable to the Truman administration's support for the moderate government of Greece in 1947 and later in Western Europe.

A final similarity between the NSS and the Truman Doctrine is the practicality to which they look to utilize the tool of economic aid. Although the United States is an idealistic nation, it is also wants to see the pragmatic results of its efforts in furthering the well being of host states. As Wiarda notes, the United States is a generous nation. However, "If they begin to see that foreign aid is being held up for political purposes by the host government, or is being wasted, or

---

[69] *The National Security Strategy of the United States of America.*
[70] Ibid.

that the relief supplies are being hoarded or sold by corrupt officials, then that generosity can dry up very quickly."[71]

In the case of the Truman administration, its doctrine clearly states that measures must be taken to assure that economic aid to Greece and Turkey is used wisely. Financial aid was given to Greece and Turkey because they cooperated with the conditions of the United States, as Truman stated, "The Greek government has also asked for the assistance of experienced American administrators, economists, and technicians to ensure that the financial and other aid given to Greece shall be used effectively in creating a stable and self sustaining economy and in improving its public administration."[72] In the closing of his speech, Truman also asked Congress to commit American civilian and military personnel to Greece and Turkey in order to assist in reconstruction, and to assure that U.S. aid was being utilized for the good of those nations.

Likewise, Bush's NSS also calls upon American pragmatism in the allotment of economic assistance. "Every project, every loan, every grant must be judged by how much it will increase productivity growth in developing countries."[73] The NSS further declares that the United States must "insist upon measurable results to ensure that development assistance is actually making a difference in the lives of the world's poor."[74] The NSS stresses that governments must fight against corruption and embrace the rule of law, in order to promote basic human rights, health care, and education. Much like the Truman Doctrine, the NSS offers economic aid as an incentive to adopt American values of democracy, economic liberalism, and human rights. This strategy has become an established norm of American foreign policy, as foreign assistance continues to translate American ideals into concrete actions that aim at assisting nations in need. Its aim is still to build a peaceful, more prosperous world.

COMPARING PRESIDENTIAL DOCTRINES

Although there are many notable comparisons between the Truman Doctrine and the Bush administration's National Security Strategy, in the context of rhetoric, foreign policy behavior, and policies, these doctrines are also strikingly different. Among the obvious contrarieties between these doctrines is the scope of foreign policy issues. First, the Truman Doctrine evolved from a congressional

---

[71] Wiarda, 42-43.
[72] *The Truman Doctrine.*
[73] *The National Security Strategy of the United States of America.*
[74] Ibid.

address, which was aimed at a specific purpose, namely economic aid to Greece and Turkey, which would secure their governments from communist insurgency. The speech was very concise and focused on a single issue. The document itself makes up between three to four pages of actual text. The Truman Doctrine was more rhetorically driven.

Second, it was not until the establishment of the Marshall Plan that the Truman Doctrine assumed the larger task of preventing Soviet expansionism throughout the European arena. Conversely, the Bush administration's NSS was an officially released policy statement. Totaling thirty pages, the security strategy covers a variety of international concerns, including global terrorism, collective international security, economic development, weapons of mass of destruction, and the threat of rogue states.

The International Environment

The most decisive contrasts between the Truman Doctrine and Bush's NSS are the international environments that produced them. The two presidential doctrines were established within fifty-five years of one another. Thus, their environmental contexts are strikingly different. Harry S. Truman held the office of president during an extremely volatile period of history that marked the transition from Word War II to the Cold War. Truman had entered the presidency during the final years of a systemic war that would result in the establishment of a new international order, which was led by the United States and the Soviet Union.

As former Secretary of State Henry Kissinger observes, "Truman inherited a political environment whose dividing lines were inchoately based on the position of armies advancing from east and west. The political fate of the countries liberated by Allied armies had not yet been resolved."[75] The United States had become an economic and military superpower after the war. As a result, it assumed the responsibility of being a world policeman, while the future of Europe lay in uncertainty. Moreover, the Truman administration had been the first to use the atomic bomb, thus heralding the nuclear age.

The Truman presidency existed in a black and white international system. After the war the world was ideologically divided between east and west, capitalist and communist. The United States had only one enemy, the communist ideology, which was embodied in the Soviet Union. The enemy of peace and security was an opposing nation-state, which had a formidable military force.

---

[75] Kissinger, 426.

However, at the time of the Truman Doctrine's promulgation, the United States still had a nuclear monopoly over the rest of the world, which gave the United States a significant upper hand in world politics.

Conversely, George W. Bush was elected as the second president of the post-Cold War era. The current international order significantly differs from that of the Cold War. Whereas, the Cold War was based on bipolarity, the current system is multi-polar and is based on interdependence. The international arena that the Bush administration faces is far more complex than that of the Truman era. In the twenty-first century, the United States must deal with a broad variety of international issues such as poverty in the third world, ethnic conflict, instability in the Middle East and Africa, and the new threats of terrorism and rogue states. These new threats to the United States and its allies are not superpower nations like the Soviet Union; as George W. Bush has stated, "The events of September 11, 2001, taught us that weak states, like Afghanistan, could pose as great a danger to our national interests as strong states."[76]

The enemy to peace and security is not a nation state with conventional military forces that employ traditional tactics. Instead, the war against global terrorism is different, as it will be fought on a number of fronts against elusive enemies over a longer period of time. In addition, the United States also faces the threat of rogue states that are acquiring weapons of mass destruction for terrorism and other acts of aggression. The NSS argues that, unlike the threat of the Soviet Union, the threat of mutually assured destruction will not deter rogue regimes whose leaders are willing to take risks. Furthermore, the United States also faces tensions with Russia and China, as these great powers still exhibit distrust towards the United States and its allies. Unlike the Truman administration, the United States faces a number of determining issues in all regions of the world, each of which have their own set of multi-faceted challenges.

CONCLUSION

Although the Truman Doctrine and President Bush's National Security Strategy are two seemingly different presidential doctrines, each of which are the products of diverse international systems, they are comparable on a number of levels. These presidential doctrines exhibit that the United States has a distinct tradition of foreign policy behavior that is a pervasive element of America's approach to foreign relations, regardless of international conditions or internal

---

[76] *The National Security Strategy of the United States of America.*

partisan politics. Furthermore, the use of economic aid to further U.S. ideals and interests has become a staple of America's foreign policy strategy. For the Truman administration, these policies have proven be successful in containing threats to U.S. security. As for the Bush administration, only time will tell.

Chapter 4

THE NIXON DOCTRINE: A NEW APPROACH TO THE CONTAINMENT STRATEGY

Richard Yon

INTRODUCTION

Presidential doctrines have been and continue to be very influential instruments in the development and execution of foreign policy goals and objectives. Throughout American history, there are numerous examples of their effectiveness and overall importance in the promotion of specific policy guidelines. When studied, they tend to highlight how a president can directly delineate the principles of foreign policy initiatives to Congress, the American people, and the world. In the following pages two presidential doctrines will be discussed and compared. The purpose is not to analyze the merits or shortcomings of the doctrines, but rather analyze the historical context and provide a description of the actual policies.

HISTORICAL ANALYSIS

In George Washington's farewell address to the nation at the end of his second term as president, he eloquently described his vision of America's role in international affairs. He warned the country of the danger of meddling in foreign matters. Washington believed that the business of the United States ought to be domestic issues and that America was blessed with the privilege of protection – in the form of "isolation" – that the Atlantic Ocean offered. The speech clearly guided U.S. foreign policy over more than a 100-year period and embodied the principles which would define the new and developing nation. Washington's farewell address became a long lasting object of guidance for successive presidents up to the twentieth century.

Instruments of Presidential Power

Many more examples exist throughout the history of presidential declarations and doctrines that consist of foreign policy and national security strategy. From the Monroe Doctrine to George W. Bush's National Security Strategy, presidents have utilized foreign and domestic policies to leave an enduring mark on the face of the country and the world. In terms of the former, the United States has gone through periods of change. As stated earlier, for many years the United States chose a passive role in international affairs from the time of George Washington to the administration of William McKinley. However, a new role emerged during the presidency of Theodore Roosevelt. Foreign diplomacy was emphasized by Roosevelt through his work on the Panama Canal, the peace agreement he fostered between Russia and Japan, as well as his decision to send the United States Navy around the world to show America's military might.

In addition to the change from a passive to an active role in foreign affairs, foreign policy decisions in the United States have proven to be a battle between Congress and the president. We have seen examples of Congress allowing the president full reign when it comes to certain issues of national security. For instance, in December of 1941 President Franklin Delano Roosevelt was confronted with the horrors of an attack by the Japanese empire on American soil. Roosevelt's speech before a joint session of Congress paved the way for his broad exercise of presidential power during World War II. However, the country has also seen instances where Congress had to be courted by the president and his administration in order to achieve certain foreign policy goals. Sometimes, this transpired with little success, as in the case of Woodrow Wilson. Shortly after the end of World War I, President Woodrow Wilson drafted a declaration to create an organization of member countries in order to prevent the worldwide calamity of war again. This organization came to be called the League of Nations. Unfortunately, Wilson's efforts did not pay off and the United States Senate – under control of the rival party – refused to approve the treaty supporting the formation of the League of Nations. In addition, Wilson failed because he did not reach out across the aisle to the Republicans in the Senate for consultation on the treaty.

Communication Tool

Perhaps one of the most important uses for a presidential doctrine has to do with its ability to function as a communication tool. The goals of U.S. foreign policy must be clearly expressed and communicated not only to the American people but also to the Congress and rest of the world. The president can also utilize the doctrine to put enemies of the United States on warning as well as build a consensus both domestically and internationally. In the initial stage in responding to the terrorist attacks of 11 September 2001, President George W. Bush effectively built a coalition internationally to support the war on terror by utilizing strong, unambiguous language. In addition, he communicated to the terrorists the intentions and fortitude of the United States.

In order to build a strong consensus and alliance backing for a presidential doctrine, the president's administration must be careful in its word selection and must also organize a campaign to sell the idea domestically and internationally. Perhaps the greatest obstacle to surmount is the partisanship of Congress. By utilizing clear and powerful language the president can garner the support of the American people and use this support to win over Congress. A perfect example of this is the effective campaign organized by President Harry S. Truman and his administration in 1947, shortly after the conclusion of World War II.

Truman had huge obstacles to overcome with his pronouncement of the Truman Doctrine. In it, he asked Congress and the American people to support the fragile governments of Greece and Turkey by supplying them with monetary aid. Truman sought aid for two reasons. The United States was the only free and democratic country at the time that could effectively offer assistance to protect these nations from the totalitarian regime of the Soviet Union. In addition, if the United States did not offer monetary aid, a serious catastrophe might likely occur in the Mediterranean, Middle East, or Asia, culminating in the dominance of the Soviet Union and the infringement on personal liberties and freedom – principles that Americans hold dear.

Truman effectively lobbied Congress and the American citizens in order to gain approval of his doctrine. His steadfast and persuasive approach, in addition to his strong and clear language, made it apparent that there was no other alternative. Inaction would be detrimental to the security of the country and the security of

U.S. allies, as well as to America's national interests overseas. This was a huge undertaking in light of the fact that the Republicans in Congress clearly opposed any involvement in foreign affairs at the end of World War II. They sought to encourage American isolationism. Moreover, Truman's popularity was low and he was facing election in 1948.

Assessing Presidential Doctrines

Presidential doctrines are significant policy agendas that can increase the power of the executive branch and greatly influence foreign policy for years to come. With carefully orchestrated wording, presidents can build a consensus, garner support for specific initiatives, and utilize the doctrines as a catalyst for change. This was clear in the re-orientation of the country in 1947 with the acceptance of the Truman Doctrine. The United States woke up from its isolationist approach to foreign policy and became more involved in international affairs.

It is important to assess the significance of each presidential doctrine in order to realize its impact on the country and successive presidents. A comparative analysis of doctrines will also highlight how each president handled particular issues and either successfully or unsuccessfully attempted to achieve the intended policy goals and objectives. By comparing and contrasting doctrines, scholars can speculate on their trends, strengths, weaknesses, and long-term effects on the United States.

NIXON DOCTRINE

During the latter part of the 1960s and the early part of the 1970s, the United States was in the midst of an international crisis. At this time, American foreign policy was characterized as a struggle between communism and democracy. The containment of Soviet expansion and totalitarianism was imperative in order to advance the ideals of democracy and secure its survival. The United States routinely supported oppressed people in governments under Soviet control in order to motivate the masses to rise up in rebellion and take back their countries and their individual freedoms. In addition, the United States provided financial aid to many countries that were targeted by the Soviets for domination. This practice was started at the end of World War II, with the provisions delineated in the Truman Doctrine, which provided aid to the governments of Greece and Turkey to counter Soviet aggression in the region. After the conclusion of World War II, the ideological war between the United States and the Soviet Union was appropriately referred to as the "Cold War."

As communism gradually gained power in Asia and the freedom and liberties of the people of that region were threatened, tensions between the ideals of democracy and communism worsened. In particular, the people of Vietnam were engaged in a civil war that exposed the country to communist domination and totalitarian control. President Lyndon Johnson recognized this as a precipitating factor for devoting American military and economic resources in the region. Further escalations led to American involvement in the Vietnam War. Johnson and his military and political advisers determined that if any concessions were made or the United States decided to withdraw from South Vietnam that a "domino effect" might occur in Asia.[77] The possibility of Thailand, Laos, Korea, and Cambodia being overtaken by communist regimes was seen as a threat to the stability in the region and in American interests abroad.

In a matter of a few years, Johnson was faced with an ongoing war with no apparent end in the near future as well as rising casualties among American soldiers. In addition, massive division and opposition to the war at home intensified the situation. Protests and peace marches were the status quo of the era and many people were disillusioned with the war effort. Not only were the citizens questioning America's involvement in Vietnam but they were also questioning America's involvement in international affairs. A blurring of the objectives of the conflict in Vietnam and the unforeseen conclusion to the war played a role in America's cynicism and apprehension over its continuation.

Johnson's decision not to seek re-election and Richard Nixon's victory in 1968 provided the new president with the grim task of inheriting the Vietnam War, America's cynicism, and its problematic foreign policy objectives. Nixon, with his clear grasp and comprehension of foreign affairs and his familiarity with international relations, realized the potential that this critical moment in history held for him and the future of America. A different strategy for foreign policy was required in order to win back the support of the American people and reposition the country's involvement in international affairs. The containment strategy that was promoted by Nixon's predecessors was responsible for America's ever increasing role in every international crisis. According to Henry Kissinger, Nixon's Secretary of State,

---

[77] Kati Marton, *Hidden Power: Presidential Marriages that Shaped Our History* (New York: Anchor Books, 2001), 159.

...Nixon perceived as his first task putting the Vietnam experience into some perspective. The United States remained essential to international stability, but it would not be able to sustain the freewheeling interventionism that had brought over 500,000 Americans into Indochina without a strategy for victory....the peace of the world depended on whether America could distinguish between those responsibilities in which its role was merely helpful and those to which it was indispensable, and whether it could sustain the latter without tearing itself apart.[78]

Between "Abdication and Overextension"

In consultation with his advisers, Nixon developed a new approach to foreign policy and sought to provide answers to America's problems in Asia. On 25 July 1969, Nixon embarked on a world trip, beginning in Guam. Nixon took this opportunity to release to the public his proposals for guiding America's involvement in international crises and his approach to foreign policy. In addition to this particular opportunity to present the Nixon Doctrine to the American people and the world, the President elaborated further on it in a speech given in November of 1969 and once again in February of 1970.[79] The Nixon Doctrine was the vehicle that Nixon utilized to back away from the containment policy of the past and usher in a new era of American foreign policy. Although Nixon realized that this was necessary in order to pull the country together, he found it difficult to completely lose his "sentimental attachment" to the containment strategy.[80] This new approach to foreign policy was different from other national security policies championed since the forties due to its multilateral framework and cooperation with other nations. The Nixon doctrine attempted to mediate between "abdication and overextension" in foreign affairs.[81] Nixon, in collaboration with Henry Kissinger, analyzed the three types of security threats in order to make a distinction about when it was right for the United States to involve itself in international matters in Asia. The three strategic areas identified by Nixon and Kissinger are as follows: "internal subversion, external attack by a neighboring Asian country, and aggression by a nuclear power."[82] Below are the integral

---

[78] Henry Kissinger, *Diplomacy* (New York: Simon and Schuster, 1994), 707.
[79] Kissinger, 1994, 708.
[80] William Safire, *Before the Fall: An Inside View of the Pre-Watergate White House* (New York: Doubleday, 1975), 153.
[81] Kissinger, 1994, 708.
[82] Henry Kissinger, *White House Years* (Boston: Little, Brown & Co, 1979), 223.

points outlined in the Nixon Doctrine that described the three criteria necessary for American involvement:

- The United States would keep its treaty commitments.
- The United States would "provide a shield if a nuclear power threatens the freedom of a nation allied with us or of a nation whose survival we consider vital to our security."
- In cases involving non-nuclear aggression, the United States would "look to the nation directly threatened to assume the primary responsibility of providing the manpower for defense."[83]

This doctrine communicated to the American people that the United States was about to embark on a new stance in regards to foreign policy, especially in Asia. The President sought more assistance from countries in particular regions to take over more of the responsibilities for intervention. The burden would be placed on threatened nations to "supply their own fighting manpower" even if the United States offered assistance and support.[84] The principles as defined in the Nixon Doctrine were eloquently elaborated on in Nixon's second inaugural address to the country:

> We shall do our share in defending peace and freedom in the world. But we shall expect others to do their share....The time has passed when America will make every other nation's conflict our own, or make every other nation's future our responsibility, or presume to tell the people of other nations how to manage their own affairs... Just as we respect the right of each nation to determine its own future, we also recognize the responsibility of each nation to secure its own future....Just as America's role is indispensable in preserving the world's peace, so is each nation's role indispensable in preserving its own peace.[85]

Nixon's second inaugural address was a defining moment in expanding the points in the Nixon Doctrine beyond Asia to other parts of the world.

---

[83] Kissinger, 1994, 708.
[84] Tom Wicker, *One of Us: Richard Nixon and the American Dream* (New York: Random House, 1991), 581.
[85] Patrick J. Buchanan, *The New Majority* (New York: The Girard Company, 1973), 50.

Vietnam

The Nixon Administration was determined not to repeat the problems associated with America's participation in the Vietnam War. The doctrine was an ideal way of ensuring that this would not happen again. According to Nixon's memoirs, the Nixon Doctrine was a new Asian policy that would simultaneously ensure American power in the Pacific region and honor existing treaties as well as make certain that any future commitments would be based on the "vital interests" of the United States.[86]

Soviet aggression and the relationship of the two superpowers during the Cold War was the major reason for the development of the containment strategy. America's global approach in foreign policy, which was necessary to carry out containment, put the United States in a precarious position. The Nixon Doctrine provided a pivotal role in re-evaluating the foreign policy initiatives of the United States, while at the same time attempting to unify the country and increase support of government actions. In addition, it offered an exit to the problematic war in Asia. However, the nature of the Cold War and America's long-standing tradition of containment made a re-orientation in international affairs very troublesome. As a leading power, the United States had responsibilities for supporting threatened nations as well as keeping the Soviet Union and the dangers of communism in check. In addition, even though the Nixon Doctrine offered an exit strategy for the war in Vietnam, Nixon also insisted that the U.S. presence in the Pacific should remain because of the nation's stature as a leading world power.[87]

In the domestic turmoil that engulfed the United States during the Vietnam War, the Nixon Doctrine was an answer to the cries against America's involvement in Asia.[88] In particular, it answered many of the divisive issues brought forth during the numerous protests and marches. America was going to continue to honor commitments in the world by living up to pre-established treaties, but it would now follow a new framework before involvement in foreign matters in Asia or any other part of the world was allowed. According to Nixon, disengagement in Vietnam would be based on the principles outlined in the Nixon Doctrine.[89]

---

[86] Richard Nixon, *The Memoirs of Richard Nixon* (New York: Grosset and Dunlap, 1978), 395.
[87] Frank Van Der Linden, *Nixon's Quest for Peace* (Washington: Robert B. Luce, 1972), 19.
[88] Kissinger, 1979, 225.
[89] Nixon, 1978, 409.

New Directions

Although the Nixon Doctrine re-oriented American foreign policy and also established new criteria for involvement, it was clearly developed specifically for Asia. After Nixon's declaration of the points prescribed to in the doctrine, Kissinger met with France's President Georges Pompidou in August of 1969. In their meeting, Pompidou professed to Kissinger that he clearly supported the new approach to Asia as outlined in the Nixon Doctrine and that he would like to see this approach utilized for Europe as well.[90] Pompidou felt that the countries in Asia and Europe should take more responsibility in matters affecting their regions and that the United States should not be in a position to continually come to the aid of other countries in matters that do not clearly affect its national security interests. Nixon eventually expanded on the doctrine in his second inaugural address to the nation where he described the doctrine's correlation with the rest of the world and America's change in its approach to foreign policy.[91] The doctrine is left open to broad interpretation.

In defense of the wording and actual substance of the doctrine, the Nixon administration contends that the ambiguity is purposeful in order to allow the United States the flexibility needed to exercise the principles of the doctrine and permit the country to be "responsive to diplomacy". A perfect example of the vague language and its effect on policy formation is the statements made by Nixon aides. In defense of the doctrine, people in the administration stated that the doctrine will not hamper American intervention in matters of national defense or fundamental interests. Instead, the new policy will call the country to examine the international arena more "precisely and prudently" to ensure proper execution of financial and military assistance.

The economic facet of the Nixon Doctrine must be assessed as well. Although the primary focus of the doctrine deals with military involvement, economic involvement should not be overlooked. As stated above, the United States sought the cooperation of other nations to absorb the costs of interregional conflicts in terms of human and monetary outlays.[92] Since the Truman Doctrine, the United States has supported threatened regimes through the allocation of monetary and military resources. With the announcement of the Nixon Doctrine, the United States wanted to create an environment in Asia that was less dependent on American support and more dependent on the resources of surrounding countries.

---

[90] Kissinger, 1979, 389.
[91] Buchanan, 1973, 50.
[92] Lloyd C. Gardner, *The Great Nixon Turnaround* (New York: New Viewpoints, 1973), 125.

Détente and Strategic Arms Control

As the Nixon administration dealt with the war in Vietnam and discontent at home due to America's interventional approach to foreign policy, it also had to contend with the issue of Soviet expansion and the ideological war that still monopolized both countries. In addition to the development of the Nixon Doctrine, the United States and specifically the Nixon administration began to embrace a new strategy beyond containment known as Détente or in the words of Henry Kissinger "peaceful co-existence" At this time, the American economy was in distress and Congress was beginning to tighten the purse strings on domestic programs and defense spending. In particular, Congress sought to decrease defense spending and employ arms control measures, which was considered by many as Congress' check on presidential authority to threaten force Domestic politics and the American economy persuaded Nixon and his advisers to evaluate and utilize Détente for the United States' benefit and national security. In addition, it allowed the United States to negotiate with their Cold War adversary and maintain a position of superiority among arms control bargaining.

At first glance, Détente was not considered the wisest option by the Nixon administration in pursuing foreign policy objectives vis-a-vis the Soviet Union. For one, it was a shift in the containment strategy, which was a highly regarded foreign policy approach that had been accepted by four previous administrations.

In addition, it expanded the role the United States would play in foreign affairs in opposition to what was delineated in the Nixon Doctrine. Nevertheless, Détente was pursued in order to ensure that the Soviet Union would not take advantage of America's economic situation. If Congress was seeking to reduce military armaments and reduce the size of the defense budget, the Nixon administration was forced to seek negotiations with the Soviet Union in order to bring about similar cuts in their armaments. By holding regular negotiations with the Soviet Union and establishing a back channel to the Kremlin for communication, the White House fed into the Soviets desire for legitimacy and ownership of its Eastern European satellite countries. In order for Détente to work successfully, the Nixon White House needed to create an environment that proved to the Soviets that they would benefit the most from the policy and in turn would be seen to weaken the United States.

As the United States and the Soviet Union embarked on negotiations over Anti-Ballistic Missiles (ABM), the benefit to the United States became apparent. Together the ABM Treaty and the SALT Agreement led to a reduction in defense sites and missile launchers for both the United States and the Soviets. However, a disparity existed between the countries and their respective military capabilities which benefited the United States. It was an extremely complex task to compare the missile forces of each country. "American missiles were smaller and more accurate; half of them were being equipped with multiple warheads (that is each missile would carry several explosive devices). Soviet missiles were larger, cruder, and less flexible."[93]

President Nixon engaged the Soviet Union in negotiations over missiles and defense sites that would have never taken place in previous administrations where policy aimed to flex muscles, operating under the mantra of "assured destruction" — deterrence based on the devastating capabilities of both countries persisted. Instead, Nixon strategically utilized the confines of domestic affairs, particularly the poor economy, to define the use of a new foreign policy tactic that benefited the United States and its objectives during the Cold War. In addition, Détente influenced the policies of successive presidents such as Gerald Ford and Ronald Reagan in the continuance of arms control negotiations and reductions which ultimately led to the end of the Cold War and the break-up of the Soviet Union.

BUSH DOCTRINE

On September 11, 2001, the United States was awakened to one of the most horrific events in American history. In a matter of minutes, America, its people, and their way of life came under the attack of radical Islamic terrorists. Many innocent people died and many heroes were born that frightful day. The terrorists tried, unsuccessfully, to hamper individual freedoms, endanger democracy, and inculcate fear into Americans' daily lives. It was a day that not only tragically affected the lives of Americans, but affected the lives of many people of different races, religions, and ethnic backgrounds from around the world. Numerous countries lost citizens in the dreadful attacks on the World Trade Center in New York City that clear September day. In response to the attack, the administration of President George W. Bush began drafting strategies to deal with this new threat to American democracy. The strategy became known as the Bush Doctrine and, later, was spelled out in the National Security Strategy of the United States.

Mobilizing Every Resource

In the doctrine, Bush details the ideals that the United States epitomizes, identifies the aggressor of 9/11, and prescribes a framework of action for actively

---

[93] Kissinger 749.

pursuing and conquering various forms of terrorism. Specifically, Bush calls for defending America and its allies from terrorism, advancing peace through the improvement of the great powers of the world, and promoting it through the democratization of different segments of society around the globe. Bush emphasized that the combination of the United States' unparalleled military strength, economic power, and international support among allies would assist the world in uncovering terrorist networks on a global scale in order to create an environment that places value on human life and "favors human freedom."[94]

The President, in his declaration of the *National Security Strategy of the United States* (Bush Doctrine), implored that every resource be engaged from homeland defense to cutting off the financial networks of terrorists in order to rid the country of the terrorist threat. Although the United States could successfully mount a global war on terror, Bush called on the nations of the world to stand up to terrorist aggression and take part in the war. The doctrine asserts that in order to achieve the goals stated above and defend the national security of the United States, America will:

- Champion aspirations for human dignity;
- Strengthen alliances to defeat global terrorism and work to prevent attacks against the U.S. and its allies;
- Work with others to defuse regional conflicts;
- Prevent U.S. enemies from threatening America, U.S. allies, and friends, with weapons of mass destruction;
- Ignite a new era of global economic growth through free markets and free trade;
- Expand the circle of development by opening societies and building the infrastructure of democracy;
- Develop agendas for cooperative action with other main centers of global power;
- Transform America's national security institutions to meet the challenges and opportunities of the twenty-first century.[95]

It is evident that the Bush administration's first and foremost concern was to safeguard America against any threat of aggression. Also, the President places great importance on the need for support from the international community in

---

[94] The National Security Strategy of the United States of America, Washington, DC: The White House. September 2002. <www.whitehouse.gov> p. 1.
[95] NSS, 5-6.

order to achieve the strategic goals established, although the extent of Bush's interest in working with other nations has been questioned by some scholars. Cooperation is key to the success of the document and its ability to garner support both domestically and internationally. However, Bush staunchly and unequivocally made clear that if a country was unwilling to support the United States in the war on terror, or if safe haven or funding was provided to terrorist networks, the United States would be prepared to take offensive action against any such country. He declared, "We will make no distinction between the terrorists who committed these acts and those who harbor them."[96]

A New Type of Enemy

The doctrine specifically highlights the fact that there was no timetable for action, nor were there any boundaries within which to operate. Terrorism is not a phenomenon that can easily be defined and contained. Instead, the terrorist network responsible for the attacks on 9/11 was one that operated in many countries, received funding from numerous sources, and did not state allegiance to any sovereign nation. In addition, Bush specifically states that the scope of the war will be global in nature and will last for an indefinite duration. In fact, this is one of the first times in U.S. history that a president has issued an order for the use of massive military force to attack an individual and his stateless network and/or organization.[97]

As acknowledged earlier, one of the major advantages of a presidential doctrine is its ability to communicate specific policy goals and objectives as well as to garner the support of all parties necessary for its successful implementation. In this case, Bush had to communicate to the American people, Congress, and U.S. allies that patience and diligence were needed in order to deal with the uncertainty that surrounded the issue at hand. Uncertainty cast a shadow on the war's duration, its geographic scope, the resources required and the possibility of future terrorist attacks. With a network permeating so many different countries and America's inexperience in dealing with this type of aggressor, the ambiguity is understandable. It was imperative that Bush address these concerns in order to provide all parties with the uncertain consequences of action. However, the Bush administration cautioned about the consequences of inaction. In his mind, there was no alternative, there was no hesitation – the safety of Americans and its democratic ideals hung in the balance. In an address to Congress and the

---

[96] Walter Lafeber, "The Bush Doctrine," *Diplomatic History* 26: 4 (Fall 2002), 543.
[97] Lafeber, 544.

American people, Bush tied America and all nations together by focusing on their joint responsibility. He acknowledged,

> This is not, however just America's fight. And what is at stake is not just America's freedom. This is the world's fight. This is civilization's fight. This is the fight of all who believe in progress and pluralism, tolerance and freedom. We ask every nation to join us.[98]

Although a multilateral approach to the war was and still is significant for its success, unilateral force would not be ruled out in order to ensure the security of the United States and protect the country from future attacks. Bush declared, in so many words, that America was running the show. He stated, "At some point, we may be the only ones left. That's okay with me. We are America."[99] Although Bush sought to build a strong coalition to fight a global war on terror, he also knew that at some point the United States might be unable to count on her allies for support. Support could be elusive for many reasons: lack of resources; unclear timeframes for commitment of those resources; and a leader's inability to maintain support from their constituents at home. It is one thing to build an effective coalition, but it takes great effort to sustain and nurture the coalition through time. It is still too early to assess the success of the doctrine or any of its particular components. As we have seen with other presidential doctrines, the success or failure and the repercussions of the doctrine will be felt for many years to come.

COMPARING THE NIXON AND BUSH DOCTRINES

In order to truly understand the implications of a presidential doctrine and its impact on domestic and foreign policy it is helpful to compare and contrast the major points of two or more doctrines. The following discussion looks at both the similarities and differences of the *National Security Strategy* (Bush Doctrine) and the Nixon Doctrine to see if any worthwhile trends are apparent. Although the Bush Doctrine is in its infancy, there is still enough substantive information to utilize in correlation with the Nixon Doctrine to assess their similar aspects as well as their differences.

---

[98] Lafeber, Walter. Pp. 553.
[99] Lafeber, 549-50.

Similarities

The major parallels that exist between the two doctrines promote the idea that presidential doctrines do have a common link. Simply by their nature as tools of communicating new policies, the similarities become apparent. For instance, both the Bush Doctrine and the Nixon Doctrine ushered in new mechanisms for handling foreign policy issues. In particular, both presidential doctrines pursued multilateral approaches to the international crises that were present. With the war in Vietnam and the war that was started on American soil with the terrorist attacks, the United States pursued the cooperation of multiple nations to bring about the goals and objectives found in the foreign policy initiatives.

A much stronger commitment to multilateralism can be seen in the Nixon Doctrine however. Although Bush was clearly committed to a coalition of nations in order to achieve the substantive goals of his Doctrine, it is apparent that he will utilize whatever means necessary (even abandoning a multilateral approach) in order to ensure America's national security. Unification was also key to the foundation of both proposals. The United States became unified shortly after the attacks on 11 September 2001 and Bush capitalized on this new found wave of enthusiasm and support for the country to carry out his agenda and fight the war on terrorism. Nixon sought to unify the country around his new foreign policy objectives of reducing American involvement in foreign affairs and providing an exit strategy to the Vietnam War.

Other similarities abound between the two doctrines. For instance, both Bush and Nixon ushered in new criteria and mechanisms for handling either the emerging or already existent international problems. In addition, their policies became very instrumental in either winning the support of the American people and the country or maintaining that support, although in the case of Nixon support waned with the Watergate scandal. The act of war was also a central concern in the policy formation. The Nixon Doctrine sought to end the war in Vietnam and make it increasingly difficult for the United States to become involved in such circumstances. The Bush Doctrine introduced the United States to a new war in which it became an unwilling partner to protect the national security of the country, weed out global terrorist networks, and ensure the survival of the American way of life.

Differences

As stated previously, war was a major component of both presidential doctrines. However, where the Bush Doctrine was concerned with a new threat (terrorism) in which the war was a global war, Nixon was grappling with a civil war in Vietnam that was isolated to Asia (even though the Cold War was global). Nixon's proposal focused mainly on Asia and Bush focused his initiative on a global scale. The main players in each instance are also different. In the case of the Nixon Doctrine, the United States was concerned with the threat of communism and Soviet expansion. Alternatively, in promoting the NSS Bush sought to neutralize global terrorist networks. As discussed earlier, these networks have no clear and distinct operating location and are not the product of any sovereign nation, whereas the Soviet Union was a distinct nation with an identifiable source (although it was expansionistic).

The topic of unity is also significant as not only a similarity but a difference as well. In the historical context of the Nixon Doctrine, the country was evidently divided over the war in Vietnam and the U.S. role in international events. Nixon's initiatives sought to bring the country together and end the divisive issues the country faced. With the introduction of the Bush Doctrine, the country was more united and supportive of the government than it had been in previous years. Bush utilized this surge in public support, approval, and unity to breathe life into his initiatives.

Perhaps the greatest and most obvious difference between the Bush and Nixon proposals are that Bush clearly intensified American involvement in international affairs. The scope of his new policy was global in terms of finding and destroying terrorist networks and supporters of the networks. Nixon, on the other hand, proposed a reduction of America's involvement internationally. In particular, he developed specific guidelines to be followed in order to determine whether America's intervention was required or necessary for the national security of the country. Although Bush sought multilateral support in regards to executing his foreign policy strategy, he did however make it quite clear that unilateral action would not be out of the question in order to accomplish specific goals. Nixon, however, specifically sought the cooperation of other nations to handle regional conflicts in order to limit America's role in international affairs and support his idea of multilateralism in regards to foreign policy.

CONCLUSION

Presidential doctrines have been an integral part of American history. Through the years, there are numerous examples of American presidents exercising their power in order to reinvent, re-orient, or completely change the strategic policy initiatives of the country. The nature of the presidency makes it extremely advantageous for presidents to utilize doctrines as a means of ensuring their place in history or significantly altering America's course of action. As we have seen, doctrines are an ideal communicating tool for garnering support for certain proposals and rallying the country behind a new course of action. From George Washington's farewell address to the nation to George W. Bush's Doctrine, as is evident in the chapters in this book, key presidential doctrines have shaped the United States. In the course of studying the cases presented in the other chapters, one can appreciate the similarities and differences that exist and the great contribution each doctrine has made. By examining the Bush and Nixon Doctrines, one can conclude that although differences may exist and decades may have transpired between them, there are still many similarities. These similarities transcend time and speak of the importance of performing comparative analyses. As we witness history and the unfolding of time, so to will we witness new presidents and new doctrines that shape and transform America while ensuring her timeless democratic ideals and freedoms.

Chapter 5

THE CARTER DOCTRINE AND NATIONAL SECURITY: AN EXAMINATION OF AMERICAN IDEALISM

Melissa Buehler

INTRODUCTION

By the time James Earl Carter, Jr. became the thirty-ninth President of the United States, much of the American public had become disillusioned with government. The domestic, as well as international, political climate was in a state of transition, as the relative strength of the United States wavered. Against these changes, Carter successfully appealed to the American public and positioned himself as a political outsider to Washington during the campaign of 1976; he was recognized as a politician that possessed strong moral and religious convictions, as well as a sense of duty to the public. After the election, the American people looked to Carter to bring a renewed sense of integrity and idealism to the Presidency. And this is exactly what Carter attempted to do: incorporate his idealism into the conduct of national security and foreign policy.

The overall effectiveness of Carter's presidency can be examined when reviewing the context in which his national security strategy developed. While this is an important element, the purpose of this chapter is to present the domestic and international environments and events that influenced Carter's national security strategy shift, rather than to analyze the causes. Many scholars have argued that Carter's lack of responsiveness, competency, and credibility influenced his foreign policy approach in 1980.[100] Instead of projecting an image of strong leadership, direction, and decisiveness, Carter's poor leadership skills fostered a sense of indecision and passivity that influenced his altered ideological approach to foreign policy. While Carter shifted his overall approach toward national security and foreign policy, he maintained his willingness to risk everything for peace, as evidenced by his efforts in the Middle East.

The administration attempted to respond to the changing domestic and international climate, as well as the declining strength of U.S. power internationally. Carter was faced with the challenge of maintaining traditional expectations of the federal government in a time of new political and economic realities. Carter's policy approach can be considered pragmatic and was designed to be responsive to the perpetual changes occurring within the international system.

In reviewing Carter's 1980 State of the Union Address,[101] a shift in his national security policy approach can be seen. Prior to 1980, Carter's national security position reflected a liberal internationalist approach that relied on diplomatic power as opposed to military strength. Following his 1980 State of the Union Address, Carter advocated an adjustment of U.S. strategy that adopted a case-by-case approach. Instead of advocating a single unified political position, this approach called for analysis of each situation. Carter's policy position departure in 1980 exemplified his indecisiveness, reinforced his lack of credibility, and provided a signal to the international community that U.S. foreign policy was in deep disarray.[102] Carter's political paralysis undermined his national security and foreign policy strategies. Ultimately, Carter failed to uphold the ideals that he attempted to enact within his doctrines.

A content analysis of Carter's 1980 State of the Union Address and President George W. Bush's National Security Strategy[103] (NSS) provides a catalyst for examining the context, scope, and purpose of the doctrines. While the differences

---

[100] Reviews consulted for chapter of Carter's foreign policy: David Skidmore, "Carter and the Failure of Foreign Policy Reform," *Political Science Quarterly* 108: 4 (Winter 1993-94), 699-729; Robert A. Strong, *Working in the World: Jimmy Carter and the Making of American Foreign Policy* (Baton Rouge: Louisiana State University Press, 2000); Joshua Muravchik, *The Uncertain Crusade: Jimmy Carter and the Dilemmas of Human Rights Policy*; I.M. Destler, "National Security Management: What Presidents Have Wrought," *Political Science Quarterly* 95, no. 4 (Winter 1980-81), 573-588.

[101] Carter's *State of the Union Address* was delivered on January 21, 1980.

[102] Skidmore, 699-729.

[103] *The National Security Strategy of the United States of America*, September 2002.

can be readily seen, several similarities surface when considering the various concepts and ideals addressed within each doctrine.

BACKGROUND

Before examining the content of the doctrines, the political, social, and economic contexts must be reviewed. The international and domestic environments will be highlighted and the main points of each doctrine will be given. Giovanni Sartori reinforces the necessity of establishing concepts and terms in comparative research.[104] As such, definitions of concepts and terms specified within the content of the chapter, as well as within the footnotes, will seek to establish nominal and operational definitions. This chapter's purpose is to demonstrate the similarities and differences between Carter's 1980 State of the Union Address and Bush's National Security Strategy through content analysis. The ideological composition, intent, and scope will be analyzed and contextually compared. The subsequent policies and overall successfulness of each doctrine will not be discussed.

An interpretative analysis of rhetoric will be used in order to compare/contrast the ideas and concepts present within each doctrine. The principles will be compared in order to establish whether or not certain American ideological concepts within foreign policy are maintained through the course of history, regardless of the international political environment, administration, social climate, and time frame.

One would assume that several concepts would transcend time and be reflected within each President's national security strategy, such as peace, domestic security, international stability, and economic security and prosperity. Through content analysis of each doctrine, the hypothesis that certain concepts transcend circumstance can be tested. By comparing Carter's 1980 State of the Union Address and Bush's NSS, the presence of differing domestic and international climates, administrations, and time frames will become evident. These elements play important roles in influencing the content and focus of each doctrine.

---

[104] Giovanni Sartori, "Concept Misformation in Comparative Politics," The American Political Science Review 64, no. 4 (Dec., 1970), 1033-1053.

The Chief Executive and National Security

The U.S. Constitution does not specifically define the role of the executive branch in reference to foreign policy formulation. This has created an ongoing struggle between the legislative and executive branches of government to influence the framing of foreign policies. While the president acts as the "commander-in-chief," the Constitution gives the legislative branch the authority to declare war. Even though the legislative and executive branches seem to share control over foreign policy, the president has maintained the fundamental responsibility of managing foreign affairs.

In the operational sense, the president is the primary foreign policy actor and sets the tone for policy formulation. The president and his advisers heavily dominate the environment in which foreign policy emerges. International issues are often where presidents feel the most accountable to the American public. Aaron Wildavsky describes several factors that enable the president to function in a relatively autonomous manner in creating foreign policy:

- Since foreign policy questions often require "fast action," they are more appropriate for executive than legislative decision making.
- Presidents have vast "formal powers to commit resources in foreign affairs," and they possess "far greater ability than anyone else to obtain information on developments abroad."
- Since voters know little about foreign policy issues, they "expect the President to act in foreign affairs and reward him with their confidence."[105]

Robert Dahl reinforces this analysis, suggesting: "In foreign policy the President proposes, the Congress disposes." He continues, "In a large number of highly important decisions about foreign policy, the Congress does not even have the opportunity to dispose."[106] Ultimately, the president must not only manage foreign policy, he must take responsibility for ensuring the success of such policies.

---

[105] Peterson, *The President, the Congress, and the Making of Foreign Policy*, 14-15.
[106] Ibid, 15.

International Relations Theory and National Security Policies

The international system can be considered decentralized and anarchic, with cooperation occurring on the basis of common interests. The external constraints of state actions are numerous. Concurrently, the process in which one would attempt to understand the relations among nations and the policies that emerge from those relationships is incredibly complex.

When considering national security policies, the necessity for guarding a nation's security, interests, and autonomy are primary goals. Kenneth Waltz states that nation-states must "worry about their survival, and the worry conditions their behavior." He continues, "Only if survival is assured can states safely seek such other goals as tranquility, profit, and power."[107] Considerable agreement can be found among international relations theories that states can be considered unitary actors. Therefore, it can be assumed that a leader who considers national interests within the context of the international system governs a nation-state. For the purpose of this chapter, the U.S. president operates as a primary actor in determining national security policies. The domestic and international environments, as well as his advisers, influence his decisions.[108]

CARTER'S NATIONAL SECURITY IDEOLOGY

During Carter's 1976 presidential campaign, an emphasis on human rights was used to rally the Democratic Party, as well as the nation. Concern for human rights effectively framed Carter's foreign policy position and unified both Democrats and Republicans on an issue that appealed across political ideology. Liberals wanted to limit U.S. support of oppressive dictators, such as Marcos in the Philippines, the Shah of Iran, and Somoza in Nicaragua. They felt that American foreign policy primarily focused on defending Cold War politics in areas of the world that did not support democratic regimes. Conservatives viewed the issue of human rights as a means of abandoning détente[109] yet criticized détente for not moderating the Soviet Union's involvement in the Third World.[110]

---

[107] Kenneth Waltz, *Theory of International Politics*, 105, 126.
[108] This is not meant to imply that the President is the only person involved in the formation of foreign policy. For the purpose of this chapter, the President acts as the primary person involved in the forming the direction of national security and foreign policy. Presidents are primary policy actors that set the tone in foreign policy.
[109] Détente was the permanent relaxation in international affairs during the Cold War, specifically between the United States, Soviet Union, and China (Strong 2000).
[110] Strong, 2000.

Carter's new foreign policy approach signaled a departure from previous détente politics.[111]

Carter's policies embodied a pragmatic strategy of adjustment that accounted for the declining global power of the United States and the unstable international power structure. The goal of this approach was to address the idea of the "Lipmann Gap," described by Samuel Huntington as "the growing imbalance between dwindling resources and static commitments."[112] The Carter administration felt that the bipolar view of world politics, as influenced by Cold War practices, insufficiently accounted for the increasing complexity of international relations. Increasing interdependence and a diffusion of power within the international arena called for an even-handed approach to U.S. foreign policy. Carter remarked during a commencement speech given at Notre Dame University in June of 1977:

> Our policy during this period was guided by two principles: a belief that Soviet expansion was almost inevitable but that it must be contained, and the corresponding belief in the importance of an almost exclusive alliance among non-Communist nations on both sides of the Atlantic. That system could not last forever unchanged. Historical trends have weakened its foundation. The unifying threat of conflict with the Soviet Union has become less intensive, even though the competition has become more extensive.[113]

Peace and Human Rights

Carter called for a new approach to American foreign policy, one that was sparked by optimism, decency, and freedom. Carter's moral ideology, as well as his liberal internationalist approach, guided his foreign policies. Three principles influenced his foreign policy: 1) peace, or the prevention of war, should be the main goal of all foreign policy practices; 2) a focus on human rights should be a necessary component of foreign policy in order to advance democracy and human dignity throughout the world; 3) and the belief that the world was too complex and large to be controlled or influenced by one or two superpowers.

---

[111] Carter stated in his 1977 commencement speech at Notre Dame University that he supported détente with the Soviet Union. His view of détente was a departure from previous thoughts of containing communism. Détente was previously used as a tool for decreasing arms buildup between the U.S. and Soviet Union. Carter viewed détente as a progress towards peace.
[112] Skidmore, 704.
[113] Jimmy Carter, *Public Papers of the Presidents of the United States: Jimmy Carter*, vol. 1 (1977), 954.

Overall, Carter's approach significantly departed from the previous Cold War paradigm. Carter felt that an exaggerated fear of communism had plagued U.S. politics for decades and a new line of communication among political leaders was necessary. New policies that were derived from a more comprehensive view of global change and international relations were necessary. Carter maintained that a primary consideration of human rights would help to foster democracy and peace, as well as extend the scope of democratic institutions and principles. Finally, Carter sought to decrease U.S. commitments in peripheral areas, such as in South Korea and rely more on diplomatic measures, as opposed to military.

International and Domestic Environment in the 1970s

Carter became president during a challenging time in U.S. history. National confidence in the federal government had been shaken following the Vietnam War and Watergate scandal. The state of the economy was compounding domestic tensions as it struggled to recover from a deep recession; and rising energy and oil prices, double digit inflation, and high unemployment rate plagued the nation.

Détente had continued to characterize U.S.-Soviet foreign relations and seemed to dominate American foreign policy during the 1970s. The ideology that framed détente seemed to diverge in reference to the practices of the United States and Soviet Union. The United States viewed détente as a means of establishing world order and managing the expansion of Soviet power; the Soviet Union viewed détente as a way of managing the transition of the United States as a super power to a more moderate role in international relations.[114] The presence of increasing Soviet strength loomed as its involvement in Third World affairs expanded, and the threat of nuclear war continued as strategic arms limitation talks (SALT)[115] with the Soviet Union stalled.

From the beginning of the Carter administration, congressional leaders accused Carter of being too soft with the Soviet Union, thus aiding its expansion. The congressional sentiment towards Carter was fueled by his announcement that he planned to withdraw all U.S. ground combat forces from Korea within five years and decrease overall military spending. Carter continued to fight criticism

---

[114] Strong, 2000.
[115] SALT was an overall political and military strategy aimed at arms reductions between the United States and Soviet Union and consisted of: " a treaty on Anti-Ballistic Missile systems; an Interim Agreement on the limitation of strategic offensive arms; a protocol to the Interim Agreement, clarifying the agreement's particulars; and, a set of common understandings regarding the ABM Treaty and Interim Agreement" (Ryan J. Barilleaux, *The President and Foreign Affairs: Evaluation, Performance, and Power*, 111-112).

that he was too weak in the area of U.S. national security. A series of events, particularly in 1979, overwhelmed Carter and added to the already heightened tensions between the United States and Soviet Union:

- In August 1979, the United States discovered Soviet troops were stationed in Cuba. This discovery led to the questioning of the competency of the CIA, Carter, and the integrity of the SALT II[116] talks.
- On October 26, 1979 the Korean CIA Director Kim Chae Kyu assassinated South Korean President Park Chung Hee, along with his Presidential Security Chief Cha Chi Chol. U.S. troop withdrawal from the Korean peninsula is halted as President Carter reaffirms the United States' commitment to its defense.
- The Soviet invasion of Afghanistan during December 1979 provided further evidence of Soviet aggression and signaled its departure from practices of détente. Carter responded with harsh rhetoric and a boycott of the upcoming Olympic games that were being held in Moscow.
- Following the Soviet invasion of Afghanistan, Carter indefinitely suspended SALT II. Carter feared that it would fail to achieve ratification by the U.S. Senate.[117]
- The Shah of Iran's removal from power signaled a changing political climate within Iran and added to the worldwide energy crisis. More than fifty U.S. diplomats were taken hostage on November 4, 1979 and held for the next 444 days. Many scholars have stated that Carter's presidency was held in hostage as well based on his extensive personal involvement.[118]

---

[116] SALT II was comprised of: "a treaty on the limitation of strategic offensive arms; a protocol to the treaty, which outlines common agreements and understandings regarding the text of the treaty; a memorandum of understanding on the establishment of a data base of monitoring compliance with the treaty; a joint statement of principles and basic guidelines for subsequent negotiations; and, a statement by the Soviet government on the Soviet Backfire bomber" (Barilleaux, 115).

[117] Carter's public approval rating was approximately 30 percent in late 1979 and greatly affected his overall political standing within the Congress. Carter's low public standing signaled a limitation in his ability to influence Congress (specifically the U.S. Senate) in accepting SALT II. The Soviet Union had also recently invaded Afghanistan, which signaled another departure from détente by the Soviets. For these reasons, Carter decided to indefinitely suspend SALT II ratification (Barilleaux, 109).

[118] Information compiled from Strong, 2000; William H. Gleysteen Jr., *Massive Entanglement, Marginal Influence: Carter and Korea in Crisis*; and Barilleaux.

During Carter's tenure, U.S. global power was threatened, in part due to the increased volatility of the international environment. This does not mean that the Carter administration did not experience any foreign policy achievements. One of Carter's greatest achievements during this time was the successful negotiation of a peace treaty between Egypt and Israel. Carter ratified the Panama Canal treaty that guaranteed its neutrality following the year 2000. Carter also continued to normalize relations between the United States and China. Finally, Carter advanced and promoted human rights within his political agenda and increased worldwide discourse concerning the issue.

The tumultuous international environment of the late 1970s influenced Carter's 1980 State of the Union Address. The content of this address reflects the increased Soviet global influence and the defensive position of the United States. Carter's address also signaled a departure from his previous national security strategy. Carter's previous attempts of rallying domestic support by emphasizing a human rights approach to foreign policy had failed. Carter's national security adjustment strategies presented a revisionist approach to defining the U.S. global power position and its goals.

Carter's 1980 State of the Union Address

In Carter's 1977 inaugural address, he called for the elimination of nuclear weapons and a greater emphasis on human rights. Carter recognized these goals as being idealistic in the face of harsh realities of a tense global environment. Nonetheless, he believed that the main goals of a nation should be "to provide more efficiently for the needs of our people, to demonstrate – against the dark faith of our times – that our government can be both competent and more humane."[119]

Carter's 1980 State of the Union Address signaled a departure from his previous treatment of Soviet expansionism but maintained his commitment to human rights. The address was designed to present the national security policies to the public in a clear manner and provide the flexibility necessary given the current crises. A portion of the speech was meant to shock the American public into a Cold War stance similar to the aftermath of the Truman Doctrine Speech of 1947.[120]

The initial context of Carter's address was that the 1980s began under circumstances of "turmoil, strife, and change" – Americans were still being held

---

[119] Carter, 1977, 954.
[120] Skidmore.

hostage in Iran and the Soviet Union was invading Afghanistan.[121] The speech addresses three distinct issues. The first and most prominent issue concerns the Soviet Union and maintenance of global security. U.S.-Soviet relations had grown increasingly strained as the Soviet Union's military continued to grow. The Soviet Union had continued to expand its global power, specifically within the Middle East and Africa.

Departing from his initial position that the world was too complex to be influenced by one or two superpower nations, Carter recognized that global symbiosis was dependent on secure relationships between the United States and Soviet Union. It was the responsibility of superpowers to exercise military restraint and promote global security; the United States had led the charge against mounting Soviet power and would continue its actions to curb Soviet expansion. Carter reaffirmed his support for the development of a cooperative security framework in establishing diplomatic solutions to resolve disputes and reiterated that peace remained the United States' primary goal. The promotion of diplomatic measures for conflict resolution would help to maintain peace and work towards the promotion of human rights and needs.

The second issue concerned the Middle East and oil. The crux of Carter's doctrine clearly established the position of the United States in regards to the stability of the Middle East and its oil resources: "An attempt by any outside force to gain control of the Persian Gulf region will be regarded as an assault on the vital interests of the United States of America, and such an assault will be repelled by any means necessary, including military force."[22] The Soviet Union posed a threat to American interests in the Middle East, and Carter questioned the intent of the Soviet Union's involvement in international matters. With their dominance of Afghanistan, the Soviets were expanding their sphere of influence, as opposed to strengthening global security and national independence.

The American hostage crisis in Iran and Soviet expansion into Afghanistan illustrated the fact that dependence on Middle Eastern oil posed a threat to the U.S. national and economic security. Carter cited the increasing prices of OPEC oil as being the main contributor to the increase in the inflation rate. Carter appealed to Congress to act on energy legislation that would promote and develop alternative fuel resources. The President also appealed to the American people to make 1980 a year for energy conservation.

The third issue addressed the strengthening of the nation's economy. Carter stated that while American material resources are great, they are in fact limited. The steps that must be undertaken in order to strengthen the economy include: a

---

[121] Jimmy Carter, *State of the Union Address*, January 21, 1980.

reduction of the deficit and a balancing of the federal budget; curb price and wage increases to counter inflationary tendencies; eliminate unnecessary federal regulation; provide job training and increase American jobs; and increase productivity, savings, and investment.

BUSH'S NATIONAL SECURITY STRATEGY

George W. Bush was the president to face the new threat of terrorism as seen through the tragedy of 11 September 2001. While the United States possessed unprecedented military, economic, and political strength, it was still vulnerable to outside threats. Adding to this threat was the fact that the "enemy" was not confined to a single state or groups of states. Relatively small cells of people could foster a sense of fear and inflict harm throughout the world. Bush's National Security Strategy is outlined within a series of speeches given by the President following the 9/11 attacks. The attacks demonstrated the reality of U.S. vulnerability. The response was widespread, as the social consciousness of the country was awakened and issues of security came into the political forefront.

Strengthening National Security

The NSS framed the U.S. national security strategy as American internationalism that was a reflection of national interests and values. The premise of the NSS is building and maintaining a "war on terrorism" in order to "help make the world not just safer but better."[122] The NSS provided an outline for strengthening national security by:

- Strengthening global alliances in order to combat global terrorism.
- Promoting the use of diplomatic measures to defuse regional conflicts.
- The promotion of economic growth through free markets and trade.
- Curb the threat and subsequent use of weapons of mass destruction, as well as the reformation of states that support terrorist activities.
- Creating a balance of power that promotes human dignity, freedom, nation building, and self-determination.
- The strengthening of global security networks through multilateral institutions.

---

[122] *The National Security Strategy of the United States of America*, September 2002.

- Aid in the development of countries by helping to establish democratic infrastructures.
- Promotion of cooperative efforts with global powers in developing comprehensive agendas.
- Supporting efforts to promote human dignity.
- Transforming American national security institutions to be responsive to the current domestic and international environments.[23]

The NSS is reflective of the changing international and domestic environments following the 9/11 attacks. It not only promotes the national security interests of the United States, it advocates the necessity for global stability, self-determination, and economic strengthening. The NSS demonstrates that all necessary measures will be utilized in order maintain U.S. security, including the use of military force.

COMPARING PRESIDENTIAL DOCTRINES

When comparing the contexts surrounding the drafting of Carter's 1980 State of the Union Address and Bush's NSS, several differences are readily seen. Aside from being drafted twenty years apart and differing in political party affiliation, the doctrines dealt with varying international climates. Carter's address occurred during a rise in Soviet power under a Cold War atmosphere. The United States was experiencing a decline in its military and political power, and the U.S. global position was not clearly defined. The U.S. economy was deeply entrenched in a time of recession and facing an energy crisis. Bush's NSS was drafted in a post-Cold War, post-9/11 environment. At this time, the U.S. global position was more clearly defined. The end of the Cold War elevated the political position of the United States as communism fell. Even though the U.S. military and political strength was established and relatively unchallenged, the 9/11 attacks demonstrated the domestic vulnerabilities that the United States faced. Compounding the threat of terrorism, the domestic and world economies were experiencing a recession following nearly a decade of economic growth and surplus.

A content analysis of the doctrines reveals several similarities as well. Both doctrines defend American interests abroad, as well as domestically. Each doctrine's content reflects the highly visible crises that occurred prior to their drafting. Carter's national security strategy was greatly influenced by the increase of Soviet power, as demonstrated by Soviet actions against Afghanistan, and the ongoing Iranian hostage situation. Bush's NSS was a direct response to the 9/11 attacks and the growing domestic terrorism threat.

Similarities between Doctrines

Even though the environments that influenced the formulation of the Carter and Bush national security strategies were different, common themes are present.

Idealism

The rhetoric used within each doctrine projects an overall sense of idealism that has been present throughout American history. They seek to embrace the ideals of morality, responsibility, democracy, and ethics; as well as the concepts that are embodied within democracy, such as liberty, peace, and justice. These ideals are present throughout the American political, social, and judicial systems. The United States has sought to uphold these concepts and instill them throughout the world. American foreign policy has sought to expand the development of other societies by helping to build democratic infrastructures throughout the world.

One of the main roles of American foreign policy has been to serve as an advocate for democracy. The principles of liberty, peace, and justice are deeply rooted within American culture. The United States has positioned itself as the champion for freedom and democracy, a defender against tyranny and oppression. The national security policies of Carter and Bush build upon this sentiment. Carter reiterates the necessity for democracy as a way of countering oppression, communism, and specifically, Soviet aggression. Carter states that the United States is committed to fighting against "colonial domination" and that the "Soviet Union must pay a concrete price for their aggression." Carter continues on to state that peace is the ultimate goal of American foreign policy and that "as a mighty nation we will continue to pursue peace." He concludes: "Together as one people, let us work to build our strength at home, and together as one indivisible union, let us seek peace and security throughout the world."

Bush's NSS begins with the idea that democracy and freedom are staples for providing for national success. The NSS clearly states, "The national security strategy of the United States must start from these core beliefs and look outward for possibilities to expand liberty." Bush recognizes that the United States currently possesses great military, economic, and political strength but:

In keeping with our heritage and principles, we do not use our strength to press for unilateral advantage. We seek instead to create a balance of power that favors human freedom: conditions in which all nations and all societies can choose for themselves the rewards and challenges of political and economic liberty. In a world that is safe, people will be able to make their own lives better. We will defend the peace by fighting terrorists and tyrants. We will preserve the peace by building good relations among great power. We will extend the peace by encouraging free and open societies on every continent.

Both the 1980 address by Carter and Bush's NSS consider the necessity for superpower nations to act responsibly in terms of military force. Carter questions the Soviet Union's actions, suggesting that they harm the collective security of the world. He states that it is the responsibility of the United States and Soviet Union to help promote a more stable international environment. Bush's NSS seeks to eradicate terrorism and free the world from any terrorist threat. The United States, acting as the hegemonic power, will work to provide a secure environment for the world at all costs.

Collective Security

Both doctrines present a broad strategic position in terms of providing global security. In order to defend peace, a sense of collective security must be achieved. Therefore, the road to peace and collective security can best be provided by democratic nations. The use of foreign economic aid and human rights are also cited as a means of promoting collective security, freedom, and democracy.

Providing collective security not only calls for diplomatic measures, such as arms control agreements, but an overall strategy for targeting impediments for peace as well. The impediments for collective security for Carter and Bush were communism and terrorism. Each doctrine addresses a type of containment approach in order to provide collective security. Carter's 1980 address advocates the containment of communism, while Bush's NSS calls for a containment of terrorism. Both doctrines seek to establish pragmatic approaches to providing for collective security. Carter cites the SALT I and SALT II negotiations, the development of national and regional alliances, the call for collective diplomatic action, the normalization of state relations with China, and the advocacy for human rights as necessities for meeting the challenges of collective security.

Bush's NSS addresses the issue of collective security in a more thorough manner. The NSS establishes several goals for collective security, such as working towards the elimination of terrorism, the continued economic development of the world economy, the development of cooperative action agendas, and the security of human rights. One of the main themes established by the NSS is that terrorism must be eradicated in every corner of the world. If terrorism occurs in one part of the world, it will bleed into other parts. The NSS recognizes that collective security cannot be provided by a single nation. Global action and the presence of alliances and multilateral institutions are necessary for its success.

A vital component of collective security is the recognition of human rights. The American approach to human rights is the necessity of freedom: freedom of religion, speech, association, and thought. The NSS states that violations against human dignity and freedom will be addressed: "We will champion the cause of human dignity and oppose those who resist it." Carter's address reaffirms the U.S. commitment to human rights as well.

Finally, both doctrines reiterate the necessity of diplomacy but stress the use of military force when necessary. The United States is not afraid to act alone if domestic, as well as collective, security is threatened. However, both doctrines illustrate that diplomatic measures are vital in maintaining global security. The development of ally networks and open communication channels are cited in both doctrines.

Economic Development

Both the Carter and Bush presidencies experienced economic recessions. The doctrines reflect the necessity for securing American economic interests and the importance of economic development. Both doctrines recognize that economic strength, as well as military strength, are important components in maintaining the U.S. global position. Global economic development aids collective security and human rights as well. Bush's NSS draws on the history of market economies by stating:

> A strong world economy enhances our national security by advancing prosperity and freedom in the rest of the world. Economic growth supported by free trade and free markets creates new jobs and higher incomes. It allows people to lift their lives out of poverty, spurs economic and legal reform, and the fight against corruption, and it reinforces the habits of liberty.

Carter echoes the primacy of secure economic interests within national security. After citing five actions necessary to strengthen the U.S. economy, Carter states:

> We will make America even stronger at home in this decade — just as our foreign and defense policies will make us stronger and safer throughout the

world. We will never abandon our struggle for a just and decent society here at home. That's the heart of America — and it's the source of our ability to inspire other people to defend their own rights abroad.

Overall, the rhetoric of both doctrines reflects the idealistic nature deeply rooted within American foreign policy. Both recognize that realistic expectations and diplomatic measures are vital for the success of their national security strategies. The Carter and Bush national security strategies can be described as tools for a "trusteeship presidency."[123] Carter and Bush developed strategies in response to specific crises and did what they felt was necessary to ensure the safety of the nation without regard for immediate public opinion or response.

The doctrines illustrate the complexities present within international relations and advocate case-by-case pragmatism. The NSS states that the United States will approach each case based on strategic principles pertaining to resource allocation, availability of external aid by other countries and institutions, and the realities of the outcome. Carter's doctrine reiterates the sentiment and calls for an adjustment strategy as well.

Differences between Doctrines

While the similarities between the doctrines are numerous, several differences exist. As stated earlier, the international environments greatly influenced the content of each doctrine. Unlike the condition experienced by Carter, George W. Bush enjoyed U.S. military, political, and economic strength that was relatively unchallenged and unprecedented. While both doctrines reflect an external threat to U.S. national security, Carter's targeting of communism specifically points to the Soviet Union. Concurrently, Bush's NSS is not confined to a single nation. It addresses terrorism on a broad level and targets rogue states, as well as individuals and conspirators.

The scope of Bush's NSS is much broader than Carter's 1980 doctrine. This can be attributed to the type of medium each doctrine was presented. Carter's doctrine was presented in his 1980 State of the Union Address to the nation, whereas Bush's NSS was formulated from a series speeches over several months. This is not meant to imply that the context of the NSS is more complex. The NSS cites one of the differences as being the threat of nuclear weapons. During the

---

[123] Charles O. Jones refers to Carter Administration as a "trusteeship presidency". The definition can be applied to characterize the actions of the Bush Administration following the 9/11 attacks. Cited in Strong.

Cold War, weapons of mass destruction (WMD) were used as a last resort. The current international environment finds the threat of WMD as a first resort.

Bush's NSS is meant to provide the framework for the war on terrorism and establishes the ideological guidelines for future foreign policies. It reiterates U.S. commitment to extending freedom and providing security throughout the world. Aside from addressing the Iranian hostage crisis, the main purpose of Carter's address is to present his newly designed position against the rising Soviet threat.

The tone of each doctrine varies as well. Sections of Carter's 1980 address are meant to be reflective of Truman's 1947speech. Carter's intent is to shock a nation into understanding the realities of a Cold War environment. Conversely, the ambitious and idealistic tone of Bush's NSS has been compared to President Woodrow Wilson's Fourteen Points doctrine. The NSS's advocacy for American leadership in the war on terrorism parallels Wilson's calls against repressive governments.

CONCLUSION

Several concepts transcend circumstance and are reflected within the national security strategies of Carter and Bush. Both doctrines reflect idealism present throughout American history. The rhetoric embodies the ideals of morality, responsibility, and democracy. The ultimate goals of U.S. national security strategies are to maintain peace and provide collective security throughout the world. Both doctrines reiterate the need for global security, advocacy for human dignity, and the promotion of democracy. Ultimately, the doctrines signaled a departure from previous foreign policy positions as they attempted to adjust to volatile international environments.

Chapter 6

THE AXIS AND THE EMPIRE: FIGHTING EVIL IN THE REAGAN AND BUSH ADMINISTRATIONS

Mark Warner

INTRODUCTION

All presidents face national security challenges during their terms in office. Only a handful, however, make national security policy choices momentous enough to influence the office and the nation for decades to come. Theodore Roosevelt forever changed the course of American history by sending forth the Great White Fleet and dramatically increasing U.S. prestige in international affairs. Roosevelt's actions commenced the transformation of America from an isolationist nation at the beginning of the twentieth century to the world's only superpower by century's end. At the conclusion of World War I, Woodrow Wilson wrote and attempted to implement his Fourteen Points. Wilson's vision for the League of Nations became the precursor to the modern United Nations. Harry Truman's legacy is in large part defined by the doctrine that bears his name. His containment policy aimed at preventing the domination of the Eurasian landmass by a hostile Soviet Union and the global spread of Communism became the foundation of American Cold War security policy that lasted forty years.[124]

---

[124] Barry Posen and Stephen Van Evera, "Reagan Administration Defense Policy: Departure from Containment," in *Eagle Defiant: United States Foreign Policy in the 1980's*. eds. Kenneth Oye, Robert Leiber, and Donald Rothchild, (Boston: Little, Brown, and Company, 1983), 70-71.

President Ronald Reagan, dissatisfied with containment, advocated a worldwide movement for freedom and democracy. The goal of the Reagan Doctrine was to rollback Marxism-Leninism up to and including its Soviet founders. During his tenure in office, Reagan was under constant attack from peace activists for his aggressive tone. It can be argued that, after Reagan's presidency, his doctrine was vindicated by the collapse of the Soviet Union and its Eastern Bloc allies and U.S. victory in the Cold War.

President George W. Bush, prompted by the terrorist attacks on New York and Washington, has formulated a similarly aggressive national security strategy. The precursor to the Bush Doctrine was announced in a televised address to the nation on the evening of 11 September 2001. President Bush stated that in the coming war on terrorism the United States would make no distinction between terrorists and those who harbor them.[125] This policy and Bush's advocacy of preemptive attack against potential adversaries, are both departures from longstanding U.S. practices. Bush followed through with his threat by launching an invasion of Iraq to drive out the regime of Saddam Hussein. This preemptive action is of such significance that when historians define the Bush Doctrine, they may well emphasize the strategy of preemptive attack, and minimize its initial focus on nations harboring terrorists. The Bush Doctrine may also signal a permanent departure from the foreign policy regime of collective security in place since Presidents Roosevelt and Truman.

The purpose of this work is to compare not just the Reagan and Bush Doctrines, but the underlying comprehensive national security strategies of the two presidents. In analyzing the similarities and differences between the two, it is interesting to compare how America's arguably two most conservative presidents elected to office since the end of World War II defined and attempted to deal with the threats confronting the American people.

CHALLENGES CONFRONTING REAGAN AND G.W. BUSH

The Reagan and Bush Doctrines were formulated under very different circumstances. Ronald Reagan's desire to triumph over the Soviet Union was a long held belief developed over decades spent in politics. Taking a tougher stance towards the USSR was a significant portion of his 1980 presidential campaign. In contrast, the Bush Doctrine was largely formulated in response to a single event, the attacks of September 2001.

---

[125] Bob Woodward, *Bush at War*, (New York: Simon and Schuster, 2002), 30-31.

Beyond Containment

Under the Truman Doctrine, relations between the United States and Soviet Union became increasingly strained. The containment policy resulted in American aid to Greece and Turkey, and the involvement of American combat forces in Korea and Vietnam. Following the Cuban Missile Crisis of 1962, however, the near miss of a nuclear confrontation encouraged both sides to pursue a more moderate course. A period of détente followed marked by superpower summits and attempts at strategic arms control negotiations throughout the 1960s and 1970s.

Certain events of the period, however, contributed to the downfall of détente. The Soviet Union engaged in a massive military buildup, seeking to become a strategic equal to the United States. The United States was enduring a number of failures that eroded American prestige in international affairs. American combat forces failed to achieve victory over communist forces in the Vietnam War. The Iranian Revolution in 1979 led to over 400 days of captivity for fifty-two American hostages. Cuban forces were actively supporting communist insurgencies on the African continent, while the Soviet Army had invaded the neighboring country of Afghanistan. This invasion was seen as a first step towards Soviet domination of the oil-rich Persian Gulf region.

Domestically, the United States was shaken by the cultural unrest of the 1960s, the Watergate scandal, and resignation of President Richard Nixon. Additionally, the U.S. economy suffered, with both inflation and unemployment in double digits for the first time in American history.[126] Assistant Secretary of State Lawrence Eagleburger described the effects on the United States in a speech to European allies:

> U.S. inability to bring the war in Vietnam to a successful conclusion, our internal torment over Watergate and subsequent paralysis in Angola, Ethiopia, and Afghanistan, culminating with the year-long agony of the hostage crisis in Iran, have undermined that confidence. Thus some wonder not only about our military power but also whether, in some profound way, we have lost the will to withstand the Soviet Union even if we have the power to do so.[127]

---

[126] Alexander Dallin and Gail Lapidus, "Reagan and the Russians: United States Policy Toward the Soviet Union and Eastern Europe," in *Eagle Defiant: United States Foreign Policy in the 1980's,* eds. Kenneth Oye, Robert Lieber, and Donald Rothchild, (Boston: Little, Brown, and Company, 1983), 200.

[127] Lawrence Eagleburger, address to the North Atlantic Assembly, Munich, Germany, October 15, 1981.

Reagan's presidential campaign of 1980 was based in large part on restoring both American morale at home and prestige abroad. His election resulted in a major shift in U.S. national security strategy. No longer content with mere containment, the Reagan Doctrine called for American aid in an attempt to rollback communism in nations where it had already taken root. Reagan's hard-line, anti-communist ideology had grown steadily throughout his career. As Screen Actors' Guild president during the 1950s, he sought to reduce the influence of Soviet sympathizers in Hollywood, while at the same time refusing to reveal names to government inquirers. His ideology grew stronger during the 1960s and 1970s, while he was both a popular conservative speaker and the governor of California.[128]

New Threats in the Post-Cold War Era

By the time George W. Bush was elected to the presidency in 2000, the threat of communism to American national security was virtually non-existent. Victory in the Cold War left the United States the world's only remaining superpower. The American economy had experienced record growth throughout the 1990s and was just beginning to slow. Debates over foreign policy by members of government often had more to do with to what extent the United States should intervene in settling regional disputes throughout the globe, rather than direct threats to American security.

The terrorist attacks on New York and Washington in September of 2001 changed the focus of America's foreign policy. Responses by previous administrations to terrorist attacks on Americans had generally been measured responses designed for retribution but not escalation. The massive number of casualties by these attacks prompted a much more comprehensive response. No longer content to attempt to contain terror networks, President Bush has reshaped U.S. national security strategy in an effort to purge humankind completely of those organizations and states who sponsor them.

Bush's desire to eliminate not only terrorist organizations, but also the regimes that support those organizations, is similar in scope to Reagan's desire to rollback communism wherever it had taken root. Both presidents advocated aggressive national security strategies designed to eliminate threats, rather than merely minimize them. Both presidents published their visions for America's role

---

[128] James Humes, *My Fellow Americans: Presidential Addresses that Shaped History,* (New York: Praeger, 1992), 254-258.

in international affairs in documents titled *The National Security Strategy of the United States of America* (NSS). President Reagan's was published in January 1988, near the end of his eight years in office. President Bush's was published in September 2002, one year after the terrorist attacks on the United States, before he was halfway through his first term in office.

THE NATIONAL SECURITY STRATEGY OF RONALD REAGAN

American relations with the Soviet Union overwhelmingly influenced Reagan's national security strategy. In his introduction to the 1988 NSS, Reagan described how the United States had fought two wars in the twentieth century to prevent the Eurasian landmass from being dominated by hostile powers. In adopting a policy of containment toward the Soviet Union, the United States was continuing a longstanding U.S. objective of maintaining an advantage in the global balance of power by having allies, rather than adversaries, in power in Europe and Asia. Reagan's enhancement to the policy of containment was the Reagan Doctrine, announced in a speech to the British Parliament in June of 1982.

> The objective I propose is quite simple to state: to foster the infrastructure of democracy – the system of a free press, unions, political parties, universities – which allows a people to choose their own way…. What I am describing now is a plan and a hope for the long term – the march of freedom and democracy which will leave Marxism-Leninism on the ash heap of history as it has left other tyrannies which stifle the freedom and muzzle the self-expression of the people.[129]

This doctrine resulted in American military and economic assistance to anti-Communist insurgencies fighting throughout the world. The Reagan Doctrine was only one part of his comprehensive national security strategy. Reagan's NSS contains five major objectives for enhancing U.S. national security.

Military and Economic Strength

Reagan's first objective was to deter any acts of aggression against the United States and its allies and, should deterrence fail, ensure that the United States would prevail in any military confrontation. He identified the Soviet Union as the

---

[129] Ronald Reagan, address to the British Parliament, London, June 8, 1982.

primary aggressor in this objective. His strategy expressly called for preventing Soviet domination of the Eurasian landmass, and preventing the transfer of advanced military technologies to the Soviet Union and its allies. Lesser goals include protecting American citizens from the threat of international terrorism, and halting the spread of nuclear weapons. Reagan also desired to decrease U.S. reliance on nuclear weapons for deterrence both by pursuing verifiable arms reduction agreements with the Soviet Union and by developing an effective strategic defense system.

Reagan's second objective concerned the American economy. He stated that a strong economy is vital to American security. The United States had grown very dependent upon foreign energy and mineral sources, so Reagan was very concerned about keeping potential supply lines open and guaranteeing access to foreign markets and foreign resources. He also desired to combat protectionism in the world economy and to promote free trade between nations.

The third objective was to find peaceful resolutions to regional conflicts throughout the world. Reagan's fear was that regional conflicts involving U.S. allies or interests would escalate to wider conflicts directly involving the United States. The President felt that regional instability was the result of actions by the Soviet Union in subverting governments and instigating communist insurgencies throughout the world. His methods for dealing with the problem included strengthening regional military alliances designed to combat the Soviets, weakening relations between the USSR and its Third World allies, and openly aiding those governments and insurgencies fighting communism.

The final two objectives were both aimed at increasing American influence throughout the world. One was to build or improve relations between the United States and friendly governments and international organizations. The President's hope was that increased feelings of goodwill towards America would result in fewer future conflicts. The second was to champion the causes of democracy and human rights throughout the world. This goal was directed both at increasing freedom inside the Soviet Union and the Eastern Bloc states and at improving human rights and democracy throughout the developing world. This objective is based upon the belief that the spread of liberal democracies throughout the world would reduce the threat of future conflict.

Security Threats

President Reagan also outlined the specific threats that he felt most endangered American national security. The primary threat was identified as the Soviet Union due to the actions it was taking to both undermine relations between the United States and American allies in Europe and to promote communist insurgencies and the implementation of authoritarian regimes throughout the developing world. He also cited the continuing military buildup by the Soviet Union and its Warsaw Pact allies, in which defense spending consumed as much as 15-17 percent of those nations' annual gross domestic product, as the principle threat to the global balance of power. The Soviet military was described as having achieved nuclear parity and numerical conventional superiority compared with NATO forces. The new directions taken by General Secretary Mikhail Gorbachev seemed to matter little. Gorbachev's policies of *glasnost* and *perestroika* were described as:

> In the Soviet Union we hear talk of "new thinking" and of basic changes in Soviet policies at home and abroad. We will welcome real changes, but we have yet to see any slackening of the growth of Soviet military power, or abandonment of expansionist aspirations. As we work to find areas for further cooperation, we will continue to judge the Soviets by their actions, rather than their words, and found our National Security Strategy on a realistic view of Soviet aims and capabilities.[130]

The primary threats from the Middle East were described in terms of the instability caused by the Iran-Iraq War and the attempts by Iran to become the dominant regional power. The Iran-Iraq War and the actions taken by each side in attacking neutral shipping threatened to hinder the supply of oil coming from the region. The United States attempted to deal with this threat by maintaining a naval presence within the Persian Gulf and by escorting neutral tankers under the American flag. Iran under the Ayatollah Khomenei was described as the most dangerous regional threat, accused of using its military capabilities and subversive propaganda to threaten American allies in the region and directly threatening American citizens with acts of kidnapping and terrorism. Iran's actions were seen through the Cold War mentality, as any actions that undermined the security of the West benefited the Soviet Union.

The third main threat came from any attempts by communists to increase their foothold in the Western Hemisphere. Insurgencies sponsored by the communist

---

[130] Ronald Reagan, *National Security Strategy of the United States*, 1988, v.

regimes of Cuba and Nicaragua threatened many of the newly formed democratic governments in Central and South America. Great emphasis was placed upon the role of the Sandinistas of Nicaragua in both oppressing their own people and exporting instability in the region. President Reagan described the danger of Soviet influence in Central America in a 1983 speech:

> Central America's problems do directly affect the security and well-being of our own people.... Two-thirds of all our foreign trade and petroleum pass through the Panama Canal and the Caribbean. In a European crisis, at least half our supplies for NATO would go through these areas by sea. It's well to remember that in early 1942 a handful of Hitler's submarines sank more tonnage there than in all of the Atlantic Ocean.... without a single base anywhere in the area.[131]

The United States combatted the spread of communism by aiding the Nicaraguan opposition, aiding the El Salvadoran government who was fighting Communist forces operating out of Nicaragua, and aiding Angolan rebels fighting a Cuban backed Marxist government. The Reagan Doctrine redefined these anti-communist insurgents as "freedom fighters," placing the Nicaraguan Contras, Afghan mujahadeen, and Jonas Savimbi's UNITA rebels in Angola on the same footing as the patriots who fought in the American Revolution, an analogy that produced mixed reviews by scholars.[132]

Objectives and Actions

Reagan's strategy called for action in three areas to achieve American national security objectives. The first area was on the diplomatic front. America continued to negotiate verifiable nuclear arms reductions with the Soviet Union. While he favored arms negotiations, Reagan did not believe as many do that arms are the reason for international tensions, stating "nations do not disagree because they are armed, they are armed because they disagree."[133] He also called for a constant barrage of international criticism directed toward totalitarian governments. The administration made constant public proclamations about the differences between democracy and totalitarianism, and increased efforts to improve the free flow of information behind the iron curtain.

---

[131] Ronald Reagan, address to the International Longshoreman's Association, Hollywood, FL, July 18, 1983.
[132] Ronald Reagan, State of the Union address, February 6, 1985.
[133] Reagan, *National Security Strategy of the United States*, 1988, 10.

The second area of action concerned economic policy. A healthy economy was viewed as fundamental to national security for a number of reasons. First, it allowed for research and development of advanced technologies that would keep the U.S. armed forces on par with their numerically superior Soviet counterparts. Additionally, a strong economy would allow for the United States, in times of crisis or war, to take full advantage of its advanced production capabilities to provide sufficient materials to ensure victory. This advantage was shown during the victories in World War I and World War II. A strong advanced economy also encourages greater education among the workforce, resulting in a deeper pool of skilled laborers and feeding further research and development.

Reagan also believed in free trade. He stated that historically the strongest economies developed from open economic systems with unrestricted trade. The transfer of goods and technology from one country to another not only increased the standard of living of both societies, but also gives the members of those societies a chance to interact and build stronger bonds of cooperation, furthering the cause of peace. Free trade was discouraged however, when it involved American adversaries. Reagan's strategy called for measures that inhibited the ability of nations such as the Soviet Union, Cuba, Libya, and Nicaragua, to participate freely in international trade.

The final area, defense policy, was the most comprehensive. It consisted of four major concepts, all geared towards deterring the Soviet Union from attacking or intimidating the United States or its allies. The defense strategy was also designed to give flexible responses to Soviet aggression, enabling adequate protection without potential catastrophic escalation. The concept of deterrence was based foremost upon the capability and willingness of the United States to use nuclear weapons to completely destroy Soviet war making capabilities. The desire to find alternate methods of strategic deterrence other than mutually assured destruction prompted the Strategic Defense Initiative.

The second goal of defense policy was reductions in nuclear arms. Reagan touted the INF Treaty signed in 1987 as an example of acceptable arms control negotiation. His first principle was that sufficient measures must be included within any negotiations to ensure that the final agreement is verifiable by both sides. Second, because of overwhelming Soviet numerical superiority in both nuclear and conventional forces, the measure of acceptability of any agreement could not be based upon equal levels of reduction but rather by how it improved American national security.

The final two areas had to do with the deterrence of conventional warfare. In dealing with the Soviet conventional threat, Reagan would rely upon NATO and other alliances, superior technology, willingness to use theaterwide nuclear weapons, and a superior economy to deter attack. The United States maintained over 300,000 deployed troops in forward NATO areas. The goal of this force was to be of sufficient size that, when combined with NATO forces present, it could thwart an attack by numerically superior Warsaw Pact forces without having to resort to nuclear weapons. The plan then called for the mobilization capability of the superior United States economy to be able to out produce the Soviet Union in terms of replacement military units and gain final victory.

THE NATIONAL SECURITY STRATEGY OF GEORGE W. BUSH

President Bush's national security strategy outlines his vision for the future of freedom and human rights throughout the world in the twenty-first century. It begins by highlighting the twentieth century victory of democracy over communism and then moves to discuss the new threat to the United States:

> Enemies in the past needed great armies and great industrial capabilities to endanger America. Now, shadowy networks of individuals can bring great chaos and suffering to our shores for less than it costs to purchase a single tank. Terrorists are organized to penetrate open societies and to turn the power of modern technologies against us. To defeat this threat we must make use of every tool in our arsenal – military power, better homeland defenses, law enforcement, intelligence, and vigorous efforts to cut off terrorist financing. The war against terrorists of global reach is a global enterprise of uncertain duration. America will help nations that need our assistance in combating terror. And America will hold to account nations that are compromised by terror, including those who harbor terrorists – because the allies of terror are the enemies of civilization.[134]

Combating International Terrorism

Bush's strategy consists of eight main points all geared towards the elimination of international terrorism and the conditions that foster it. They range from rooting out terror organizations abroad to revamping homeland security, from championing human rights to spurring worldwide economic prosperity. NSS reflects the belief that radical ideologies tend to take strongest root in poverty-stricken areas of the world. It also reflects the notion that liberal democracies tend to not go to war with each other, so the best chance for worldwide peace is the

---

[134] George W. Bush, *The National Security Strategy of the United States of America*, 2002, iv.

spread of liberal governments with market based rather than centrally dictated economies.

Bush's first directive is for the United States to "champion aspirations for human dignity" throughout the world. The United States is opposed to the imposition or existence of totalitarian governments. Protecting human dignity includes establishing and maintaining the necessary foundations for democracy, such as free speech, freedom of religion, ethnic tolerance, equal protection under the law, respect for women, and respect for private property. The primary methods of championing the cause of human dignity will be through attempting to influence worldwide public opinion and through American foreign assistance. American financial assistance will be given to those struggling non-violently for political and religious freedom.

The second pillar of the Bush national security strategy is the defeat of global terrorism and the prevention of attacks against the United States and its allies. NSS states that regardless of the grievances that any group in the world may have, no cause justifies terrorism – which is defined as the premeditated, politically motivated violence perpetrated against innocents. One of the goals of the United States is to generate an international dialogue with the end result being consensus in the international community that places terrorism on equal footing with slavery and genocide, acts that are universally condemned. Bush also desires to reduce the potential for terrorist regimes such as the Taliban in Afghanistan to ever again take hold of a nation by working more closely with moderate Muslim regimes and by encouraging more open flows of information to that part of the world.

The actual war on terrorism targets terrorist organizations of global reach and organizations or terrorist states that have indicated a desire to acquire weapons of mass destruction (WMD). In a departure from traditional American policy, Bush has indicated a willingness to make preemptive strikes if necessary, and act without the support of the international community if necessary, rather than waiting for another attack to occur. This change to a first strike philosophy and targeting of nations that acquire WMD was demonstrated by the war in Iraq. As to whether or not the same philosophy will be used to eventually target and topple the other two regimes in Bush's proclaimed "Axis of Evil" – North Korea and Iran – it is too early to tell at the time of this writing, but most scholars doubt the President will attack these regimes.

Other Security Threats

The third goal of the Bush strategy is to "work with others to defuse regional conflicts." Ironically enough, this goal reflects Bush's campaign attacks on the Clinton administration for using the American armed forces for "nation building." One desire of this goal is to build regional organizations that can deal with local crises when they occur. The second desire of this goal is for the United States to only spend resources attempting to help those who truly want to help themselves. Limited American resources, including time, troops, or prestige, are no longer to be spent in areas that do not reflect national priorities. When Bush was campaigning and first took office, he expressed little desire to become involved in the Israeli-Palestinian conflict, often stating that those two sides needed to come up with their own timetable for peace, feeling that one imposed by the United States had little chance of long-term success.

The fourth objective of the Bush national security strategy is to protect the United States and its allies from WMD. Bush explains how the threat has changed from the "mutually assured destruction" of the large nuclear arsenal of the Soviet Union to the threat posed by rogue states possessing nuclear, chemical, or biological weapons. Rogue states are defined as those who display no regard for international law, mistreat their own citizens, sponsor international terrorism, hate the United States, and are determined to acquire WMD. They are said to be even more dangerous than the Soviet Union because they are less likely to be deterred than the more rational Soviets were at the threat of their own destruction. Additionally, whereas nuclear weapons were the weapons of last resort during the Cold War, they are likely to be the weapon of choice should they be acquired by rogue states. The two rogue nations specifically identified are North Korea and Iraq.

Bush also sees global economic growth as a way to strengthen national security. The President believes that as economies improve, citizens are less likely to embrace radical ideologies and engage in acts that potentially threaten their prosperity. America's free market economy should serve as the example for developing nations to emulate to lift their citizens out of poverty. Specific policies that should be encouraged in all nations' economies include: pro-growth policies that encourage outside investment; low tax rates; the intolerance of corruption so common in Third World nations; a market driven economy; improved education; and free trade. The United States can assist developing nations by improving stability in emerging markets and by continually encouraging and expanding free trade.

The sixth goal of the Bush national security strategy is to "expand the circle of development by opening societies and building the infrastructure of democracy." The concept behind this goal is that future American economic aid will be tied to political and market reform within the nations receiving assistance. Similar to his complaints about many American domestic programs, Bush laments that past results have been measured by the amount of money spent in foreign assistance rather than by how much the lives of the citizens of recipient nations have been improved.

Despite vows that the United States will act unilaterally if it is deemed necessary, President Bush recognizes that "there is little of lasting consequence that the United States can accomplish in the world without the cooperation of its allies and friends in Canada and Europe." He emphasizes the important role that alliances play in the war on terrorism and desires to expand and strengthen NATO, and to strengthen Pacific alliances with Japan, South Korea, and Australia. Improved relations with Russia, India, and China will not only help wage the war on terror, but will also serve to move those countries closer to desired economic reforms and eventually in the case of China, desired political reforms and improvements in human rights.

The final stated objective of Bush's national security strategy is to "transform America's national security institutions to meet the challenges and opportunities of the twenty-first century." The national security institutions to which the NSS refers includes the armed forces, intelligence gathering agencies, and the State Department. America's armed forces have trained since the end of World War II to fight large-scale battles against regular armed forces. The new strategy calls for an emphasis on rapid deployment to any part of the globe, no matter how remote. In rethinking military strategy however, Bush reemphasizes the importance of never allowing any nation to reach military parity with the United States. He desires to have a military so much more powerful than any other in the world that any potential adversary would be too discouraged by the gap in military might to even contemplate an arms race.

The intelligence gathering community of the United States also needs to redirect efforts from its historical Cold War role, as more emphasis needs to be placed on intelligence gathering to assist the war on terrorism. The role of the Department of State will be enhanced as part of implementing the NSS. State Department diplomats will serve as advisers in nations where reforms implementing democracy and free market economies are being undertaken. Similarly, it will fall upon the diplomats of the State Department to educate the Muslim world on American values and ideals to ensure that the voices of terror leaders describing America are not the only ones being heard. Bush describes the war on terrorism as a battle for the future of the Muslim world. The State Department will be vital in ensuring that the public relations portion of the battle leans in America's favor.

COMPARING PRESIDENTIAL DOCTRINES

Similarities

The national security strategies of Presidents Reagan and G.W. Bush have a number of similarities. First, both represented a dramatic escalation from the policies of previous administrations. Both presidents based their strategies on a desire to eliminate, rather than contain, the primary threat to American security. Both presidents were willing to take the steps they felt were essential for American security with or without broad coalitions of international support. Reagan and Bush also believed that using blunt language to point out the abuses of totalitarian regimes was completely appropriate in international affairs, as evidenced by Reagan's labeling of the Soviet Union as the "Evil Empire" and Bush's description of Iraq, Iran, and North Korea as the "Axis of Evil."

The strategies of Reagan and Bush both had trouble winning over European public opinion. Reagan's deployment of Pershing II nuclear missiles in Germany came with the support of Western European leaders, but caused massive public protests in the era of the nuclear freeze movement. Bush generally found much support in the war on terrorism, but in the war against Iraq the President encountered strong opposition from the leaders of France and Germany. Many Europeans, for a variety of reasons, viewed both Reagan and Bush as bigger threats to peace than either the Soviet Union or Iraqi dictator Saddam Hussein.

Both strategies are based upon the fundamental belief that, given the chance to compete, the American system will prevail in the world. The principles of liberal democracy, free markets, free trade, free flow of information, and human dignity will always take root and gain the support of the citizenry if not suppressed by totalitarian dictatorships. The Reagan Doctrine is founded upon this belief. George W. Bush aggressively expanded the Reagan Doctrine by using the American military to replace totalitarian regimes in both Afghanistan and Iraq.

Finally, Ronald Reagan and George W. Bush each believed the deployment of ballistic missile defense to be vital to American security. Reagan's Strategic Defense Initiative was both hailed as visionary and met with overwhelming skepticism about its cost and feasibility. However, SDI did have a significant impact on the Soviet's assessment of their capabilities and relative strength compared to the United States. Bush has formally withdrawn the United States from the ABM Treaty with Russia, and intends on deploying at least a limited system as soon as possible. Fear of a potential rogue state missile attack following September 11 has muted criticism of missile defense deployment.

Differences

Separated by fourteen years and dramatic changes in world politics, the national security strategies of Presidents Ronald Reagan and George W. Bush have many important differences. The first and most obvious difference is in defining the nature of the threat. In Reagan's estimation, the Soviet Union and the expansion of communism posed the greatest threat to the United States. Soviet expansion and aggression was responsible for regional conflicts, economic stagnation, and suffering by hundred of millions forced to live under communist rule. The massive Soviet military buildup of the 1960s and 1970s prompted Reagan's desire to rebuild the United States military once in office. For President Bush, terrorist attacks on the United States served to define the major threat. Reagan's crusade against communism is definitely matched at least in initial intensity by Bush's crusade against international terrorism and state sponsors of terror.

Potentially the most significant and lasting difference is the strategy of preemption adopted by George W. Bush. Until the terrorist attacks of 9/11, American strategy throughout the twentieth century was one of self-defense. Reagan adhered to longstanding American tradition in stating "The United States does not start fights. We will never be an aggressor."[135] Bush's fear of a repeat of 9/11, but with weapons of mass destruction, has led to a new strategy. Bush's NSS states "Given the goals of rogue states and terrorists, we can no longer rely on a reactive posture as we have in the past…We cannot let our enemies strike first."[136] Bush believes that the Cold War concept of deterrence is no longer acceptable for twenty-first century threats.

In Southwest Asia, the two presidents see the primary threat differently. For Ronald Reagan, the primary threat to U.S. security came from Iran. He was only a few years removed from the overthrow of the Shah's pro-American government by the century's first Islamic fundamentalist regime under the Ayatollah Khomenei. American memories of hostages held in Iran and being taken by Iranian backed groups in Lebanon, contributed to Iran's labeling as the bigger

---

[135] Ronald Reagan, address to the nation, March 23, 1983.
[136] Bush, 2002, 14-15.

threat. By the time George W. Bush had taken office, Khomenei was dead and the United States had already fought one war against Iraq. Saddam Hussein had invaded Iran and Kuwait, had used chemical weapons, and continued to support Palestinian, if not al-Qaeda, terrorists. Although Iran had been included as part of Bush's "Axis of Evil," Iraq was thought of as the greater threat.

Bush's strategy seems much more international in its scope than Reagan's. His economic plans give much more detail on how to improve the economies of all nations, whereas the Reagan Doctrine seems far more concerned with keeping the U.S. economy strong. Bush's reasoning seems to be based in a belief that by raising nations out of poverty, the United States will prevent breeding grounds for future extremism. Bush's attempts to reach out to other nations may also be based upon the need for their assistance in the fighting the war on terrorism. In Reagan's era, the United States knew exactly where to find its enemy, the same is not true for Bush.

Reagan's NSS takes a much more lecturing tone towards Congress, at one point lamenting "the increasing tendency of Congress to act in a directive manner with regard to details of foreign, defense, and arms control policy, limiting the flexibility of the executive branch by enacting into law positions on which the president should be allowed reasonable discretion." At another point he states "the reluctance on the part of Congress to provide the financial resources necessary to support our National Security Strategy is a cause for rising concern."[137] Bush's NSS does not even mention Congress. This may be a product of the point in time in which each strategy was adopted. George W. Bush's plan was adopted one year following the attacks on America, while Taliban and al-Qaeda forces in Afghanistan were being routed, and his popularity remained strong. Although many of the actual policies were already in practice, Ronald Reagan's strategy was published following the Iran-Contra scandal, an event that had severely weakened his presidency.

Another interesting difference exists in stating which groups fighting for freedom will be rewarded with American aid. The foundation of the Reagan Doctrine is that the United States will provide aid to anti-Communist insurgencies throughout the world. Bush's objective is different. Aware that in world opinion, one group's freedom fighters may be another group's terrorists, Bush only pledges assistance to those working for freedom in a non-violent manner.

Major differences also exist concerning weapons of mass destruction. Reagan is only moderately concerned with proliferation. His main concern is with the large arsenal possessed by the Soviet Union. He favors seeking arms control

---

[137] Reagan, 1988, 37-41

agreements that reduce nuclear weapons, but only addresses chemical and biological weapons in the context of the Soviets have them, so we must have them as a deterrent. Bush does not seem at all concerned with the fact that the Russians have nuclear weapons, but rather that they may not do a good job keeping track of them. One of the foundations of his entire national security strategy is the prevention of a nuclear weapon falling into the hands of a rogue state or terrorist organization.

Finally, the Arab-Israeli conflict is also seen differently by the two presidents. Bush feels that it is a regional issue, and that the two sides have to be willing to work together to achieve peace before any American involvement can be meaningful. Although he seems to be more critical of and makes more demands upon the Palestinian side, he also makes demands upon Israel, probably in part to gain needed Arab support in the war on terror. Bush has required that the Palestinians hold elections as a condition for American support for their statehood. Reagan saw the difficulties in the Middle East within the context of relations with the Soviet Union. Unrest was due to communist subversion encouraged by the Soviets. Even when the Soviets were not involved, he felt that anything that reduced Western influence or required Western nations to spend time or resources indirectly benefited the USSR in its struggle with the United States.

Conclusion

America's two most conservative presidents since World War II faced similar challenges against very different foes. Ronald Reagan's lifelong anti-communism was implemented as the foundation of his national security strategy. His crusade once in office is thought by some to be responsible for the collapse of the Soviet Union and U.S. victory in the Cold War. George Bush had his crusade forced upon him after his election. After eighteen months, he remains as determined as was Reagan to have the United States prevail in its latest struggle. If America succeeds quickly in its war on terrorism, Bush may be remembered as Reagan is, as the president who achieved victory over a mighty adversary. If the struggle takes decades to resolve, Bush may be remembered, as is Harry Truman, as the president who established the national security principles for the next generation. Should Bush lose focus and falter, he could be remembered as Lyndon Johnson, the only American president to lose a war.

Conclusion

There are potentially several methodological approaches one might employ toward the study of presidential doctrines. This book has examined presidential doctrines and American foreign policy from a more normative approach, selecting several case studies and comparing the ideas espoused by two primary sources. Important presidential doctrines of the twentieth century were selected as case studies and examined. The examination included comparison of the various presidential doctrines with George W. Bush's *National Security Strategy* (which arguably will form the basis of the "Bush Doctrine").

The book has highlighted the fact that significant dissimilarities exist between the various doctrines. This should not be surprising given that each president from Woodrow Wilson to George W. Bush dealt with differing domestic and international conditions, which significantly influenced their respective doctrines and approaches to foreign policy. However, despite these circumstantial inconsistencies, each presidential doctrine shares striking similarities that transcend domestic and international conditions to reflect the core principles and values of American foreign policy. Idealistic values such as international free trade, collective security, self-determination, and the leadership of the United States are espoused by each of the doctrines discussed, and are epitomized in the Fourteen Points of Woodrow Wilson, where our study of presidential national security doctrines began.

A HISTORY OF NATIONAL SECURITY CHALLENGES

Establishing a New National Security Regime

Woodrow Wilson's Fourteen Points is the final doctrine of what can be seen as the first twentieth century "national security regime," which was forged under the presidencies of William McKinley and Theodore Roosevelt. By the conclusion of World War I, Wilson fashioned his Fourteen Points doctrine hoping it would serve as the guiding light for a new era of global peace and stability. Wilsonian principles of universal equality and liberty are reflective of the morality that Americans attach to foreign policy. In turn, this idealism is the product of the American experience. As a result of the United States' success as a democratic and economically liberal nation, Americans have viewed and still view themselves as the model for building a peaceful and prosperous nation. Therefore, Americans look to export these values to the rest of the world. In his Fourteen Points, Wilson held the United States as the centerpiece of world politics, stating that American values of justice, liberty, and security are "universal."

The ultimate failure of the League of Nations and the onset of World War II caused many to dismiss Wilsonian principles as unrealistic and impossible. By the conclusion of World War II, the United States emerged as an economic and military superpower. In the midst of this elevation in power and influence, a second national security regime emerged under the presidencies of Franklin D. Roosevelt and Harry S. Truman. At the same time, however, this new foreign policy regime embraced many of the key points of the idealistic Fourteen Points such as free trade, collective security, and American leadership. These principles were affirmed in a 1941 address to Congress, in which Franklin D. Roosevelt outlined the Four Freedoms:

> In the future days, which we seek to make secure, we look forward to a world founded upon four essential freedoms. The first is freedom of speech and expression-everywhere in the world. The second is freedom of every person to worship God in his own way-everywhere in the world. The third is freedom from want-which, translated into world terms, means economic understandings, which will secure to every nation a healthy peace time life for its inhabitants-everywhere in the world. The fourth is freedom from fear-which translated into world terms means a worldwide reduction of armaments to such a point and in such a thorough fashion that nation will be in position to commit an act of physical aggression against any neighbor-anywhere in the world.

Roosevelt's Four Freedoms were reflective of Wilsonian principles. In an effort to expand upon the Wilsonian legacy, Roosevelt sought to create an international organization to replace the failed League of Nations. The United Nations would prove to be more enduring than the League of Nations. The organization would be much stronger than its predecessor, as its charter would be regarded as international law. Roosevelt would not live to see the establishment of the United Nations or the Allied victory over the Axis powers. The task of completing the conflict and establishing the post-war order would be left to Roosevelt's successor, Harry S. Truman.

Collective Security and the Post-War Order

Of the twentieth century presidents, Harry S. Truman's presidency was among the most difficult. His administration saw the completion of World War II, the start of the Cold War, and the Korean War. The Truman Doctrine, and its counterpart the Marshall Plan, set a new precedent in American foreign policy as it committed American economic aid to nations who were threatened by communism. This policy would become a permanent fixture of American foreign policy during and after the Cold War. The Truman Doctrine's policy of economic assistance would prove to be an effective method for exporting American values and institutions. The Truman Doctrine and the Marshall Plan would also establish the policy of containment, which would be the centerpiece of Cold War foreign policy. In addition to seeing the establishment of the United Nations, the Truman administration also established the North Atlantic Treaty Organization (NATO), which placed the United States and Western Europe in a collective security alliance. The NATO alliance would carry on even after its primary threat, the Soviet Union, disintegrated. The Truman administration would complete the legacy started by Roosevelt. By the conclusion of Truman's presidency, a new national security regime was in place.

The Roosevelt/Truman national security regime remained intact through the presidencies of Dwight D. Eisenhower, John F. Kennedy, and Lyndon B. Johnson. The regime withstood the strain of the Cuban Missile Crisis and the escalation of the Vietnam War. It was not until the Presidency of Richard M. Nixon that the established foreign policy order would be revised, as the United States would seek to ease tensions with its archrival in the policy of Détente.

The primary focus of the Nixon Doctrine was to withdraw the United States from its long and taxing involvement in Southeast Asia. The administration did not abandon containment, but modified it. Under the Nixon Doctrine, the United

States expected other nations to do their part in the fight against communism, specifically to commit manpower. Forging an exit strategy for Vietnam was the underlying principle behind the Nixon Doctrine. However, the administration still displayed its willingness to check Soviet Power and would provide a nuclear shield to any nation allied with the United States. The establishment of the Nixon Doctrine called for the United States to be more observant of international conditions and more prudent in the allocation of its financial and military resources. Under the guidance of Henry Kissinger, the Nixon administration's foreign policy would gear itself more in the direction of "realpolitik" (practical politics and realism).

Watergate eventually undermined many of the Nixon administration's efforts. After Nixon's impeachment, Vice President Gerald R. Ford took office. The Ford administration's foreign policy was a continuation of the Nixon legacy, as Henry Kissinger retained his position as Secretary of State. Domestically, as a result of the scandals of the Nixon administration coupled with a long and arduous campaign in Vietnam, the American public was disillusioned and distrustful of the political establishment. Internationally, the United States status as a superpower had begun to waver. It was during this time – and, to a degree, a result of these events – that Jimmy Carter won the office. Carter's approach to foreign policy differed from that of his predecessors in that he believed the fear of communism was exaggerated thus and hindered the development of American foreign policy. Remnant of Wilsonian principles, Carter believed that peace should be the goal of all foreign practices and that the promotion of human rights would foster peace and democracy. Additionally, Carter relied more upon diplomacy as opposed to military intervention.

Although Carter's strategy varied from the hawkish policies of containment and bipolar balance-of-power politics, it still possessed fundamental values of American foreign policy such as moral responsibility, the promotion democracy, and human rights. Like previous presidential doctrines, the Carter Doctrine sought to expand the development of other nations through the promotion of democracy.

Ultimately, Carter became a "lame duck" president, as his administration was bogged down by the Iranian hostage crisis. Moreover, Soviet actions including the invasion of Afghanistan and increase of its armaments production, signaled the continuing threat of conflict. Carter's successor would take a more aggressive approach toward the Soviet Union and the implementation of American foreign policy.

Unlike his predecessor, Ronald Reagan did not believe that communism was an exaggerated threat. Since his days in the film industry, Reagan was suspicious of communism, and especially of the Soviet Union. Reagan's foreign policy had little use for Détente, as he identified the Soviet Union as the aggressors. Reagan's primary strategy was to roll back communism and deter the Soviets, which he would do through collective security alliances and providing aid to states and insurgent groups fighting against communism. In the event that these methods failed, Reagan wanted to ensure that the United States would triumph in a military dispute. Thus, Regan would increase defense spending and reinitiate the arms race.

Although Reagan's tactics were far more aggressive than previous presidents, his doctrine is laden with the rhetoric and values that been salient throughout the presidential doctrines discussed. Similar to other doctrines, Reagan's doctrine affirms the importance of free trade and the belief that healthy economies promote peace and stability. Reagan's speeches often described America as a great country and a leader of the free world. In terms of the moral crusade, America was righteous, while the Soviet Union was an "evil empire." Although Regan was out of office by the time the Soviet Union collapsed in 1991, many argue that he played a significant role in ending the Cold War.

THE PRESENT NATIONAL SECURITY ENVIRONMENT

The end of the Cold War saw a dramatic change in the very nature of the international system. The Soviet Union had dissolved while its former satellite states struggled to modernize and join the West. The international arena was no longer dictated by a bipolar power struggle between the superpowers. This era was marked by a less structured and more interdependent environment. In the midst of the Soviet collapse, the United States faced new problems such as regional conflicts, international terrorism, and the threat of rogue nations. The vestiges of the Cold War era would be tested by these new problems, as exemplified in the collapse of Yugoslavia and the many localized disputes it spawned. This crisis in the Balkans would bring about the first NATO mission, nearly fifty years after the organization's inception. Likewise, the United Nations would engage in numerous peacekeeping and humanitarian efforts in Africa and Asia. Despite these new challenges, the national security regime set forth by Roosevelt and Truman remained securely intact through the post-Cold War presidencies of George H.W. Bush and Bill Clinton. During this period the United States experienced unparalleled economic prosperity and military dominance.

The international landscape would once again change as a result of the terrorist attacks of 11 September 2001. The United States and the rest of the world now faced the harsh reality of international terrorism. The attacks displayed how an underground, fundamentalist organization could inflict damage equal to that of a nation state. Nevertheless, *The National Security Strategy of the United States* (the Bush Doctrine), would reaffirm the values and policies expounded by previous doctrines from Woodrow Wilson to Reagan. Addressing a large range of issues including free trade, self-determination, collective security, and democracy, the NSS keeps in with the traditions of American foreign policy. The doctrine's commitment to assisting the AIDS crisis in African is no less idealistic and morally conscious than Wilson's Fourteen Points or the Carter Doctrine.

Although rhetorically the Bush Doctrine is consistent with the foreign policy behavior of its forerunners, the recent war in Iraq has caused many to question the endurance of the Roosevelt/Truman regime. Although history reveals that Operation Enduring Freedom is not the first time the United States has engaged in a campaign without the support of the United Nations or its allies, some have suggested that the relatively hawkish unilateralism exhibited by the administration is an attempt to dismantle the foreign policy regime established by Roosevelt and Truman. Is the United States at the dawn of a new national security regime? Are the institutions, processes, and approaches that defined collective security through a half century no longer relevant? Or, will the present regime survive the challenges of the current administration, as it had done so with previous presidencies?

The first national security regime of the twentieth century lasted nearly fifty years. If regime changes occur in cycles, then it is a possibility that we are on the verge of a change. However, such notions are merely speculative at this point, as history needs to take its course. Although it is certain that the next national security regime, whenever it may occur, will possess the idealistic values and principles that have guided American foreign policy and national security since the United States emergence as a great power over one hundred years ago.

APPENDIX A: PRESIDENTS

Presidents	**Years**	**Party**
1. George Washington	1789-1797	No party
2. John Adams	1797-1801	Federalist
3. Thomas Jefferson	1801-1809	Democratic-Republican
4. James Madison	1809-1817	Democratic-Republican
5. James Monroe	1817-1825	Democratic-Republican
6. John Quincy Adams	1825-1829	Democratic-Republican
7. Andrew Jackson	1829-1837	Democrat
8. Martin Van Buren	1837-1841	Democrat
9. William Henry Harrison	1841	Whig
10. John Tyler	1841-1845	Whig
11. James K. Polk	1845-1849	Democrat
12. Zachary Taylor	1849-1850	Whig
13. Millard Fillmore	1850-1853	Whig
14. Franklin Pierce	1853-1857	Democrat
15. James Buchanan	1857-1861	Democrat
16. Abraham Lincoln	1861-1865	Republican
17. Andrew Johnson	1865-1869	Union
18. Ulysses S. Grant	1869-1877	Republican
19. Rutherford B. Hayes	1877-1881	Republican
20. James A. Garfield	1881	Republican
21. Chester A. Arthur	1881-1885	Republican
22. Grover Cleveland	1885-1889	Democrat
23. Benjamin Harrison	1889-1893	Republican
24. Grover Cleveland	1893-1897	Democrat
25. William McKinley	1897-1901	Republican

Presidents	Years	Party
26. Theodore Roosevelt	1901-1909	Republican
27. William Howard Taft	1909-1913	Republican
28. Woodrow Wilson	1913-1921	Democrat
29. Warren G. Hardin	1921-1923	Republican
30. Calvin Coolidge	1923-1929	Republican
31. Herbert Hoover	1929-1933	Republican
32. Franklin D. Roosevelt	1933-1945	Democrat
33. Harry S. Truman	1945-1953	Democrat
34. Dwight D. Eisenhower	1953-1961	Republican
35. John F. Kennedy	1961-1963	Democrat
36. Lyndon B. Johnson	1963-1969	Democrat
37. Richard M. Nixon	1969-1974	Republican
38. Gerald R. Ford	1974-1977	Republican
39. Jimmy Carter	1977-1981	Democrat
40. Ronald Reagan	1981-1989	Republican
41. George Bush	1989-1993	Republican
42. Bill Clinton	1993-2001	Democrat
43. George W. Bush	2001-	Republican

APPENDIX B: PRESIDENTIAL DOCTRINES

Doctrine	Year	Event
Monroe Doctrine	1823	European intervention in Latin America. • Delivered at Monroe's 7th annual message to Congress (2 December 1823). • Initially conceived in response to Russian interest in the Pacific Northwest. • Called on European powers to end attempts to colonize the Americas and not interfere in Latin America. • Established the western hemisphere as the exclusive sphere of influence for the U.S.
Roosevelt Corollary	1904	European intervention in Latin America. • Expanded Monroe Doctrine to include protecting U.S. citizens and property and promoting U.S. foreign policy in the hemisphere. • Instability among Latin American states entitled the U.S. to intervene the internal affairs of these states to protect U.S. interests in the hemisphere.
Wilson's Fourteen Points	1918	World War I. • Designed to promote a lasting peace and just order following WWI. • Outline for post-war cooperation among states issued at address before joint session of

Doctrine	Year	Event
		Congress (8 January 1918): 1. Abolition of secret diplomacy; 2. Freedom of the seas; 3. Removal of trade barriers; 4. Reduce armaments; 5. Resolve colonial disputes to satisfaction of both colonial government and population; 6. Evacuation of Russian territories; 7. Evaluation and restoration of Belgium; 8. Evacuation and restoration of France and French territories; 9. Readjust Italian territories; 10. Autonomy for people of Austria-Hungary; 11. Evacuation of territories of Serbia, Montenegro, and Romania; 12. Self-determination for non-Turkish peoples under Turk control; 13. Independent Poland; 14. Establish an "association of nations".
Roosevelt's Four Freedoms	1941	World War II • Expression of U.S. world view and intention to promote these values delivered at annual message to Congress (6 January 1941): 1. Freedom of speech; 2. Freedom of religion; 3. Freedom from want; 4. Freedom from aggression.
Truman Doctrine	1947	Soviet influence in Greece and Turkey. • Initially designed to send U.S. aid to anti-communist forces in Greece and Turkey. • U.S. supports countries threatened by communist subjugation. • "Containment" of Soviet expansionism.

Appendix C: U.S. Wars (Declared)

Doctrine	Year	Event
Eisenhower Doctrine	1957	Suez War and Middle East stability • U.S. will intervene militarily in the Middle East to protect against spread of communism

Nixon Doctrine	1969	Vietnam War
		• Military and economic assistance to nations allied with U.S. against communism.
		• U.S. support of nations whose security threatened by communism (Southeast Asia, Persian Gulf, Israel).
		• Tenets for U.S. action:
		  1. Honor all treaties in responding to invasion of lands of U.S. allies;
		  2. Provide nuclear umbrella to world against nuclear threat of other nations;
		  3. Provide military assistance (weapons, technical assistance) but do not commit troops to local conflicts.

Carter Doctrine	1980	Soviet invasion of Afghanistan. • In response to the Soviet invasion of Afghanistan in 1979, Carter delivered a pledge to contain Soviets during his State of the Union Address (1980). • Any Soviet aggression toward Persian Gulf nation treated as attack on U.S. interests.
Reagan Doctrine	1980s	Communist insurgencies in Latin America. • An alternative to "containment," which was seen as a failure, designed to combat "Brezhnev Doctrine" of Sovietization of Third World. • "Roll back" and Soviet influence and defeat Soviet Union.
Clinton Doctrine	1990s	Ethnic and nationalistic conflict. • In the post-Cold War world, nuclear war and Soviet aggression are no longer the primary threats to security.

Doctrine	Year	Event
		• U.S. will act through diplomacy and force to curb ethnic violence around the world.
		• Human rights violations can be punished.
Bush NSS (Doctrine)	2001	Terrorist attacks.
		• U.S. has the right to use pre-emptive strikes against any state that threatens U.S. security.
		• U.S. will not distinguish between terrorists and states supporting terrorists.

APPENDIX C: U.S. WARS (DECLARED)

War	*Years*	*Enemy*
Revolutionary War (War for Independence)	1775-1783	Great Britain
War of 1812	1812-1814	Great Britain
Mexican War	1846-1848	Mexico
Civil War	1861-1865	Union v. Confederacy (11 southern states)
Spanish-American War	1898	Spain
World War I	1917-1918	Germany & Austria-Hungary
World War II	1941-1945	Axis (Germany, Italy, Japan)

Appendix D: Presidential Use of Military Force (Not Including Declared Wars)

In Africa (Sub-Saharan)

Date	Place	Description
1820-1823	West coast	Navy enforces 1819 Slave Traffic Act
1843	Ivory Coast	Navy fights pirates and slave traders
1851	Johanns Isl.	Navy protects U.S. whaling interests
1860	Angola	Protects U.S. citizens during civil unrest
1964	Congo	U.S. military support to government against insurgents
1967	Congo	U.S. military support to government against insurgents
1978	Zaire	U.S. military support to government against insurgents
1990	Liberia	Protect U.S. embassy, evacuate U.S. citizens from unrest
1991	Zaire	Aircraft transport French/Belgian troops, evacuate U.S. citizens
1992	Sierra Leone	Evacuate U.S. citizens/others during coup
1994	Rwanda	Evacuate U.S. citizens/others during civil unrest
1996	Liberia	Evacuate U.S. citizens/others during civil unrest
1996	Rwanda	U.S. military supports humanitarian relief/refugees
1997	Congo	Protect U.S. citizens/others during civil unrest
1997	Gabon	Protect U.S. citizens/others during civil unrest
1997	Sierra Leone	Evacuate U.S. citizens/others after army mutiny
1998	Guinea-Bissau	Evacuate U.S. citizens/others after army mutiny
1998	Kenya	Troops deployed for security after U.S. embassy bombings
1998	Tanzania	Troops deployed for security after U.S. embassy bombings
1998	Liberia	Provide security/evacuation after civil unrest

IN ASIA

Date	Place	Description
1832	Sumatra	Navy punishes Sumatrans for plundering U.S. ship *Friendship*
1838-1839	Sumatra	Navy punishes Sumatrans for attacking U.S. ships
1843	China	Marines land after fighting between U.S.-Chinese traders
1853-1854	Japan	Commodore Perry displays naval force in region
1854-1855	China	Protect U.S. interests during civil unrest
1855	Hong Kong	U.S. forces fight pirates
1856	China	Protect U.S. interests during British-Chinese hostilities
1859	China	Navy protects U.S. interests
1863	Japan	U.S.S. *Wyoming* retaliates against attack on U.S. ship *Pembroke*
1864	Japan	Protect U.S. Minister during negotiations with Japan
1864	Japan	U.S. and international forces compel Japan to allow shipping
1866	China	Punish an assault on U.S. consul
1867	Formosa	Navy burns huts as punishment for murdering shipwrecked citizen
1868	Japan	Protect U.S. interests during civil war
1871	Korea	Punish attacks against U.S. interests/murder of crew of ship
1888	Korea	Protect U.S. residents during civil unrest
1894-1895	China	Marines stationed for Sino-Japanese War/troops protect citizens
1894-1896	Korea	Protect U.S. citizens during Sino-Japanese War
1898-1899	China	Protect citizens/consulate during political unrest
1900	China	Protect U.S. citizens during Boxer Rebellion
1904-1905	Korea	Protect U.S. citizens during Russo-Japanese War
1911-1912	China	Protect citizens/consulate during revolution
1912-1941	China	Frequent U.S. landings/protection of U.S. interests during unrest
1920-1922	Siberia	Marines guard U.S. radio station on Russian Island
1945	China	Over 100,000 U.S. troops in China after WWII
1948-1949	China	Protect U.S. citizens/embassy after communist takeover
1950-1953	Korea	Korean War; over 300,000 U.S. troops
1950-1955	Taiwan	Navy prevents communist attack on Formosa/vice versa
1954-1955	China	Evacuate U.S. citizens from Tachen Islands
1962	Thailand	Marines land to support against threat of communist takeover
1962-1975	Laos	Troops support anti-communist forces

Appendix D: Presidential Use of Military Force

Date	Place	Description
1964-1973	Vietnam	Vietnam War; 543,000 U.S. troops
1970	Cambodia	Troops clean out communist operation bases
1975	Vietnam	Evacuate U.S. personnel and refugees
1975	Cambodia	Evacuate U.S. personnel and refugees
1975	South Vietnam	Evacuate U.S. personnel and refugees
1975	Cambodia	U.S. forces retake S.S. *Mayaguez* after Cambodian naval seizes it
1976	Korea	Additional forces sent in after U.S. personnel killed in DMZ
1989	Philippines	U.S. forces defend government against coup; protect U.S. embassy

IN EUROPE

Date	Place	Description
1827	Greece	U.S. landing parties hunt pirates
1849	Smyrna	Navy gains release of citizen captured by Austrians
1851	Turkey	Display of force in Mediterranean after massacre of Americans
1858-1859	Turkey	Display of force in Mediterranean after massacre of Americans
1912	Turkey	Troops guard U.S. citizens during Balkan War
1918-1920	Russia	Protect U.S. citizens during war (Czech-Bolshevik)
1919	Croatia	Troops help police fighting between Italians and Serbs
1919	Turkey	Marines guard U.S. consulate during Greek occupation
1922	Turkey	Protect U.S. citizens during civil unrest
1941	Greenland	U.S. takes Greenland under its protection during WWII
1941	Iceland	U.S. takes Iceland under its protection during WWII
1946	Italy	U.S. transport plane shot down by Yugoslavia; troops deployed
1948-1949	Berlin	U.S. airlifts supplies after Soviet blockade of city
1974	Cyprus	Evacuate U.S. citizens during Turk-Greek Cypriot fighting
1985	Italy	Navy pilots intercept airliner carrying PLO terrorists
1993	Bosnia	U.S. airdrops supplies to Muslims surrounded by Serb forces
1993-1999	Bosnia	U.S. planes/troops participate in NATO action to stop war
1994	Macedonia	U.S. troops support NATO action to stop war
1997-1998	Albania	Evacuate U.S. citizens/others and secure U.S. embassy

IN LATIN AMERICA/CARIBBEAN

Date	Place	Description
1798-1800	Dominic.Rep.	Naval/land war with France after privateering
1806	Mexico	U.S. platoon invades briefly
1822-1825	Cuba	Navy suppresses pirates
1824	Puerto Rico	Town occupied briefly to suppress pirates
1831-1832	Malvinas Isl.	Forces protect U.S. citizens during maritime dispute
1833	Argentina	Protect U.S. citizens during civil unrest
1835-1836	Peru	Protect U.S. citizens during civil unrest
1836	Mexico	Territory dispute during Texas insurrection
1842	Mexico	U.S. military occupation
1844	Mexico	Border dispute
1852-1853	Argentina	Protect U.S. citizens during civil unrest
1853	Nicaragua	Protect U.S. citizens during civil unrest
1859	Mexico	Army pursues Corina into Mexico
1860	Colombia	Protect U.S. citizens during civil unrest
1865	Panama	Protect U.S. citizens during civil unrest
1866	Mexico	Protect U.S. citizens during civil unrest
1867	Nicaragua	Marine occupation
1868	Uruguay	Protect U.S. citizens/customhouse during civil unrest
1868	Colombia	Protect passengers/treasure in transit
1870	Mexico	Destruction of the pirate ship *Forward*
1873	Panama	Protect U.S. citizens during civil unrest
1873-1896	Mexico	Army crosses border in pursuit of criminals
1876	Mexico	Temporary policing in town of Matamoros
1885	Panama	Guard items in transit during revolution
1888	Haiti	Force displayed to convince government to release U.S. ship
1890	Argentina	Protect U.S. citizens/consulate during civil unrest
1891	Haiti	Protect U.S. citizens during civil unrest
1891	Chile	Protect U.S. citizens/others during revolution
1894	Brazil	Protect U.S. shipping/interests during civil war
1894	Nicaragua	Protect U.S. citizens/interests during revolution
1895	Colombia	Protect U.S. interests during attacks by bandits
1896	Nicaragua	Protect U.S. citizens during civil unrest
1898	Nicaragua	Protect U.S. citizens during civil unrest
1899	Nicaragua	Protect U.S. citizens during civil unrest
1901	Panama	Protect U.S. property/keep transit lines open during civil unrest

Appendix D: Presidential Use of Military Force

Date	Place	Description
1902	Colombia	Protect U.S. citizens during civil war
1902	Panama	Prevent landing of Colombian troops
1903	Honduras	Protect U.S. citizens/interests during civil unrest
1903	Dominic. Rep.	Protect U.S. citizens/interests during civil unrest
1903-1914	Panama	Protect U.S. interests/Panamanians during war for independence
1904	Dominic. Rep.	Protect U.S. citizens/interests during civil unrest
1906-1909	Cuba	Restore order/protect civilians after revolution
1907	Honduras	Protect U.S. citizens during war between Honduras and Nicaragua
1910	Nicaragua	Protect U.S. citizens/interests during civil unrest
1911	Honduras	Protect U.S. citizens/interests during civil war
1912	Honduras	Prevent seizure of U.S.-owned railroad by government
1912	Panama	Supervise elections
1912	Cuba	Protect U.S. citizens/interests during civil unrest
1912-1925	Nicaragua	Protect U.S. citizens/interests during civil unrest
1913	Mexico	Evacuate U.S. citizens from Yaqui Valley
1914	Haiti	Protect U.S. citizens during civil unrest
1914	Dominic. Rep.	Stopped bombardment of Puerto Plata
1914-1917	Mexico	Occupation of Veracruz
1915-1934	Haiti	Maintained order during political instability/civil unrest
1916-1919	Mexico	Pursued revolutionaries into Mexico
1916-1924	Dominic. Rep.	Maintained order during civil unrest
1917-1922	Cuba	Protect U.S. citizens/interests during civil unrest
1918-1920	Panama	Supervised elections
1919	Honduras	Maintained order in neutral zone during civil war
1920	Guatemala	Protect U.S. citizens/interests during civil unrest
1921	Panama/ Costa Rica	Prevent war (Panama and Costa Rica) over boundary dispute
1924	Honduras	Protect U.S. citizens/interests during election hostilities
1925	Honduras	Protect civilians during civil unrest
1925	Panama	Protect U.S. citizens/interests during civil unrest
1926-1933	Nicaragua	Protect U.S. citizens/interests during coup d'etat
1933	Cuba	Protect U.S. citizens/interests during civil unrest
1940	Caribbean	Protect British air/naval bases during WWII
1954	Guatemala	Military aid to anti-Arbenz forces
1959-1960	Caribbean	Protect U.S. citizens/nationals during Cuban crisis
1962	Cuba	Support Cuban exiles in Bay of Pigs Invasion
1965	Dominic. Rep.	Protect U.S. citizens/civilians during civil unrest
1981	El Salvador	Trained government forces in counterinsurgency

Date	Place	Description
1983-1989	Honduras	Military training and maneuvers
1983	Grenada	Protect U.S. citizens; restore order
1986	Bolivia	Assist in anti-drug operations
1989	Panama	Capture/arrest of Gen. Manuel Noriega
1989	Colombia/Bolivia/Peru	Military aid/advising for drug eradication
1993	Haiti	Enforce UN embargo
1994-1996	Haiti	Enforce UN embargo; peacekeeping mission

IN THE MIDDLE EAST

Year	Place	Description
1801-1805	Tripoli	Marines free crew of the *Philadelphia*
1815	Algeria	Navy attacks Algiers in second Barbary War
1815	Libya	Navy secures indemnities for offenses in War of 1812
1882	Egypt	Navy secures U.S. interests during British invasion
1903	Syria	Protect U.S. consulate/diplomats during uprising
1948	Palestine	Protect U.S. diplomats during hostilities
1956	Egypt	Evacuate Americans during Suez crisis
1958	Lebanon	Marines invited to help protect government during insurrection
1976	Lebanon	Evacuate Americans/Europeans during civil war
1980	Iran	American planes unsuccessfully try to rescue U.S. hostages
1981	Libya	Navy planes shoot down Libyan jets over Gulf of Sidra
1982	Egypt	Multinational force in Sinai for Egyptian-Israeli peace treaty
1982	Lebanon	Marines try to restore Lebanese government after civil war
1982	Lebanon	Marines help withdrawal of PLO forces after Israeli invasion
1983	Egypt	AWACS planes sent in response to Libyan hostility in Sudan
1984	Persian Gulf	AWACS planes sent to help Saudis during Iran-Iraq War
1986	Libya	Navy missiles attack Libyan targets
1986	Libya	Bombing strikes against Libyan terrorist/military facilities
1987-1988	Persian Gulf	Navy re-flag/escort Kuwaiti oil tankers during Iran-Iraq War
1989	Libya	Navy jets shoot down Libyan jet fighters in Mediterranean
1990	Saudi Arabia	Troops deployed to Saudi Arabia to protect from Iraqi invasion

1991	Iraq	Armed forces join coalition to remove Iraqi troops from Kuwait
1991	Iraq	Armed forces deployed to protect Kurds from Iraqi military
1992	Kuwait	Troops sent to Kuwait after Iraq refuses to cooperate with UN
1992-2003	Iraq	Armed forces enforce no-fly zones in Iraq
1993	Iraq	Armed forces shoot down Iraqi jets; destroy Iraqi anti-aircraft guns
1993	Iraq	Navy bombs Iraqi military site after assassination attempt on Bush
1998	Afghanistan	Airstrikes against terrorist facilities after U.S. embassies bombed
1998	Sudan	Airstrikes against terrorist facilities after U.S. embassies bombed
1998	Iraq	Iraqi industrial sites bombed/prevent weapons of mass destruction
2001-2002	Afghanistan	Invasion to remove Taliban regime and terrorists
2003	Iraq	Invasion to remove regime and terrorists

IN THE PACIFIC

Date	Place	Description
1840	Fiji Islands	Punish islanders for attacking U.S. explorers
1841	Drummond Isl.	Punish islanders for murdering U.S. seaman
1841	Samoa	Punish islanders for murdering U.S. seaman
1855	Fiji Islands	Punish islanders for attacking U.S. citizens
1858	Fiji Islands	Punish islanders for murdering U.S. citizens
1870	Hawaiian Isl.	U.S. forces land at Honolulu
1874	Hawaiian Isl.	Protect U.S. residents during government transition
1888-1889	Samoa	Protect U.S. citizens during civil war
1889	Hawaiian Isl.	U.S. forces intervene in revolution
1893	Hawaii	Marines land to force a change in government
1899	Samoa	Protect interests during civil unrest
1899-1902	Philippines	U.S. defeats Spain; conquer Filipinos; troops stationed in islands

Note: Adapted from Karl R. DeRouen, Jr., *Historical Encyclopedia of U.S. Presidential Use of Force, 1789-2000* (Westport, Conn.: Greenwood Press, 2001); Richard Grimmet, *Instances of Use of U.S. Armed Forces Abroad, 1798-1999* (Washington, D.C.: Congressional Research Service Report, 1999).

BIBLIOGRAPHY

Allen, Neal, "The Fight Against Terror in Historical Context," in *America's War on Terror* edited by Patrick Hayden, Tom Lansford, and Robert P. Watson (England: Ashgate Publishers, 2003).

Bagby, Wesley M. *America's International Relations Since World War One* (New York: Oxford University Press, 1999).

Barrilleaux, Ryan J. *The President and Foreign Affairs: Evaluation, Performance, and Power* (New York: Praeger, 1985).

Bennett, G.H. *The American Presidency, 1945-2000: Illusions of Grandeur* (New York: Sutton Publishing, 2000).

Blechman, Barry, and Stephen Kaplan. *Force Without War* (Washington: Brookings Institution Press, 1978).

Boot, Max, "Doctrine of the 'Big Enchilada,'" *Washington Post* (14 Oct. 2002), A29.

Boyer, Paul, "Some Sort of Peace: President Truman, the American People, and the Atomic Bomb," *The Truman Presidency* edited by Michael J. Lacey (New York: Cambridge University Press, 1991), 174-190.

Buchanan, Patrick J. *The New Majority* (New York: Girard Co., 1973).

Bush, George W. *The National Security Strategy of the United States* (September 2002).

Carter, Jimmy. *Public Papers of the Presidents of the United States: Jimmy Carter* vol. I (1977).

Combs, Jerald A., and Arthur G. Combs. *The History of American Foreign Policy*, 2nd ed. (New York: McGraw-Hill, 1997).

Daalder, Ivo H., James M. Lindsay, and James B. Steinberg, "The Bush National Security Strategy," Policy Brief #109 (Washington: Brookings Institution, 2002).

Dallin, Alexander, and Gail Lapidus, "Reagan and the Russians: United States Policy Toward the Soviet Union and Eastern Europe," in *Eagle Defiant: United States Foreign Policy in the 1980s* edited by Kenneth Oye, Robert Lieber, and Donald Rothchild (Boston: Little, Brown, 1983), 191-236.

Destler, I.M. "National Security Management: What Presidents Have Wrought," *Political Science Quarterly* 95: 4 (Winter 1980-81), 573-588.

Diggins, John Patrick, ed., *The Liberal Persuasion: Arthur Schlesinger, Jr. and the Challenge of the American Past* (Princeton, N.J.: Princeton University Press, 1997).

Elliot, Michael, "The Trouble with Saving the World," *Time* (30 Dec 2003 – 6 January 2003).

Gardner, Lloyd C. *The Great Nixon Turnaround* (New York: New Viewpoints, 1973).

Gleysteen, William H. *Massive Entanglement, Marginal Influence: Carter and Korea in Crisis* (Washington, D.C.: Brookings Institution Press, 1999).

Goldstein, Judith, and Robert O. Keohane. *Ideas & Foreign Policy: Beliefs, Institutions and Political Change* (Ithica, N.Y.: Cornell University Press, 1993).

Hayden, Patrick, "The War on Terror and the Just Use of Military Force," in *America's War on Terror* edited by Patrick Hayden, Tom Lansford, and Robert P. Watson (Hampshire, England: Ashgate Publishing, 2003).

Humes, James. *My Fellow Americans: Presidential Addresses that Shaped History* (New York: Praeger, 1992).

Keohane, Robert O., and Joseph S. Nye. *Power and Interdependence* (New York: Longman Publishers, 2001).

Kissinger, Henry. *Diplomacy* (New York: Simon & Schuster, 1994).

_____. *White House Years* (Boston: Little, Brown, 1979).

Knock, Thomas. *To End All Wars* (1992).

Kuniholm, Bruce R., "U.S. Policy in the Near East: The Triumph and Tribulations of the Truman Administration," *The Truman Presidency* edited by Michael J. Lacey (New York: Cambridge University Press, 1991), 301-315.

Lackey, D. *The Ethics of War and Peace* (Englewood Cliffs, N.J.: Prentice Hall, 1989).

LaFaber, Walter, "The Bush Doctrine," *Diplomatic History* 26: 4 (Fall 2002).

Landau, Saul. *The Dangerous Doctrine: National Security and U.S. Foreign Policy* (Boulder, Colo.: Westview Press, 1998).

Latham, Earl. *The Philosophy and Policies of Woodrow Wilson* (Chicago: University of Chicago Press, 1958).

Link, Arthur S. *The Higher Realism of Woodrow Wilson, and Other Essays* (Nashville, Tenn.: Vanderbilt University Press, 1971).

_____. "The Higher Realism of Woodrow Wilson," *Journal of Presbyterian History* XLI (March 1963), 2.

_____. *Wilson the Diplomat* (Baltimore: Johns Hopkins University Press, 1957).

Link, Arthur S., and William M. Leary, Jr. *The Diplomacy of World Power: The United States, 1889-1920* (New York: St. Martin's Press, 1970).

Martin, Kati. *Hidden Power: Presidential Marriages that Shaped Our History* (New York: Anchor Books, 2001).

McDougall, Walter. *Promised Land, Crusader State* (1997).

Messer, Robert L. *The End of an Alliance: James F. Byrnes, Roosevelt, Truman, and the Origins of the Cold War* (Chapel Hill: University of North Carolina Press, 1982).

Mollenhoff, Clark R. *The President Who Failed: Carter Out of Control* (New York: Macmillan Publishing, 1980).

Moore, John L. *President Carter, 1978* (Washington, D.C.: CQ Press, 1979).

Muravchik, Joshua. *The Uncertain Crusade: Jimmy Carter and the Dilemmas of Human Rights Policy* (New York: Hamilton Press, 1986).

Nixon, Richard. *The Memoirs of Richard Nixon* (New York: Grosset and Dunlap, 1978).

Offner, Arnold A. *Another Such Victory: President Truman and the Cold War, 1945-1953* (Stanford, Calif.: Stanford University Press, 2002).

Orend, B., "Justice After War," *Ethics and International Affairs* 16 (2002): 43-56.

Peterson, Paul E., ed. *The President, the Congress, and the Making of Foreign Policy* (Norman: University of Oklahoma Press, 1994).

Pfiffner, James, and Roger H. Davidson, eds. *Understanding the Presidency* (New York: Longman Publishers, 2003).

Posen, Barry, and Stephen Van Evera, "Reagan Administration Defense Policy: Departure from Containment," in *Eagle Defiant: United States Foreign Policy in the 1980s* edited by Kenneth Oye, Robert Leiber, and Donald Rothchild (Boston: Little, Brown, 1983), 67-104.

Powaski, Ronald E. *Cold War: The United States and the Soviet Union* (New York: Oxford University Press, 1998).

Rice, Dondoleeza, "Campaign 2000: Promoting the National Interest," *Foreign Affairs* (Jan/Feb. 2000), 45-62.

Rosati, Jerel A. *The Politics of United States Foreign Policy*, 2nd ed. (Fort Worth, T.X.: Harcourt Brace, 1999).

Rosenberg, Emily. *Spreading the American Dream: American Economic and Cultural Expansion* (New York: Hill and Wang, 1975).

Safire, William. *Before the Fall: An Inside View of the Pre-Watergate White House* (New York: Doubleday, 1975).

Sartori, Giovanni, "Concept Misinformation in Comparative Politics," *American Political Science Review* 64:4 (Dec. 1970), 1033-1053.

Shull, Steven A. *Domestic Formation: Presidential – Congressional Partnership* (Westport, Conn.: Greenhaven Pres, 1983).

Simpson, Christopher. *National Security Directives of the Reagan and Bush Administrations: The Declassified History of U.S. Political and Military Policy, 1981-1991* (Boulder, Colo.: Westview Press, 1995).

Skidmore, David, "Carter and the Failure of Foreign Policy Reform," *Political Science Quarterly* 108: 4 (Winter 1993-1994), 699-729.

Skowronek, Stephen. *The Politics Presidents Make: Leadership from John Adams to Bill Clinton* (Cambridge, Mass.: Belknap Press of Harvard University, 1997).

Strong, Robert A. *Working in the World: Jimmy Carter and the Making of American Foreign Policy* (Baton Rouge: Louisiana State University Press, 2000).

Thompson, Margaret C., ed. *President Carter* (Washington, D.C.: CQ Press, 1977).

Van Der Linden, Frank. *Nixon's Quest for Peace* (New York: Grosset and Dunlap, 1978).

Waltz, Kenneth N. *Theory of International Politics* (New York: McGraw-Hill, 1979).

Wiarda, Howard J. *American Foreign Policy: Actors and Processes* (New York: HarperColins, 1996).

Wicker, Tom. *One of Us: Richard Nixon and the American Dream* (New York: Random House, 1991).

Wildavsky, Aaron, "The Two Presidencies," in *Perspectives on the Presidency* edited by Aaron Wildavsky (Boston: Little, Brown, 1975).

Woodward, Bob.*Bush at War* (New York: Simon and Schuster, 2002).

CONTRIBUTORS

Melissa J. Buehler is a Ph.D. student at Purdue University. Her research focuses on international law, human rights, and the presidency, and she is co-authoring a work on Thomas and Martha Jefferson.

Charles Gleek is a completing his M.A. degree at Florida Atlantic University in 2004 and palns to pursue his Ph.D. His research interests are in world politics, global security, international law, peace and conflict, and American foreign policy. Gleek co-authored an article on the Electoral College and presented papers at the meetings of the International Studies Association and Western Social Science Association.

Michael Grillo is completing his M.A. degree at Florida Atlantic University in 2004 and is planning on pursuing his Ph.D. His field of study is international relations, with a specialization in comparative politics. His main areas of interest include ethnic conflict, nationalism, and the effects of religion on international relations. He presented a version of this paper at the 2003 meeting of the Western Social Science Association.

Mark Warner is a Ph.D. student at Florida International University studying American Politics with a specialization in U.S. National Security Strategy. Warner served eleven years as an officer in the U.S. Navy.

Robert P. Watson, Ph.D. is Associate Professor of Political Science at Florida Atlantic University and Editor of the journal *White House Studies*. The author or editor of 17 books, Watson has published over 100 scholarly articles on the presidency and American politics. A frequent media commentator, he has been interviewed by CNN, MSNBC, *USA Today*, and numerous other media outlets, appeared on C-SPAN's *Book TV* program, and directed the first-ever "Report to the First Lady," which was presented to the White House. Watson has been a visiting scholar at many universities, presidential libraries, and historic presidential sites and foundations, and serves on the boards of several academic journals and associations.

Richard Yon is a graduate student at Florida Atlantic University. His areas of interest are presidential studies and American politics. Yon's research has focused on such topics as presidential doctrines, Thomas and Martha Jefferson, presidential health care initiatives, and the American criminal justice system. He has presented papers at the Western Social Science Association and the International Lincoln Center's conference on Thomas Jefferson, has a chapter forthcoming in the book *Debating the Issues: American Government and Politics* (Longman Publishers), and served as an assistance with the Truman Legacy Symposium held at the Harry S. Truman Little White House in Key West. Yon will continue his academic career by pursuing his doctorate in political science.

INDEX

#

11 September 2001 (9/11), ix, 19, 20, 21, 26, 32, 35, 41, 61, 69, 71, 73, 87, 88, 89, 92, 96, 109, 117

A

Adams, President John Quincy, 3, 119
Afghanistan, x, 8, 12, 21, 29, 33, 53, 56, 84, 86, 88, 97, 105, 108, 110, 116, 123, 133
Allen, Neal, 17, 20, 22
al-Qaeda, 21, 22, 110
American foreign policy, x, 1-6, 25-28, 39, 41, 42, 49-52, 54, 62, 64, 67, 81-83, 89, 92, 113, 115, 116, 118, 139
American government, 3, 109
American intervention, 67
American people, 19, 33, 59, 61, 63-65, 71, 73, 77, 86, 96
Anti-Ballistic Missile Treaty (ABM Treaty), 21, 68
Anti-Ballistic Missiles (ABM), 34, 68, 83, 109
anti-Soviet views, 42
anti-terror campaign, 22
assassination, 133
Atomic Energy Commission, 45
Axis powers, 42, 44, 115

B

balance of power, 30, 35, 51, 87, 90, 99, 101
bin Laden, Osama, 21
Bosnia, 8, 10, 129
Boxer Rebellion, 128
Brookings Institution, 1, 12, 26, 135, 136
budget, 68
Bulgaria, 43, 45
Bush administration, ix, 20, 21, 33, 35, 37, 50, 54, 55, 56, 57, 70, 71
Bush Doctrine, x, 19, 20, 26, 69, 70, 71, 72, 73, 74, 96, 113, 118, 136
Bush, President George H.W., 18, 20, 117
Bush, President George W., ix, x, xi, 5, 6, 8, 12, 13, 16, 18, 19, 22, 26, 32, 39, 41, 42, 49, 50, 51, 52, 56, 60, 61, 69, 75, 78, 87, 92, 96, 98, 104, 108, 109, 110, 113, 120, 135
Bush's National Security Strategy, x, xi, 26, 42, 49, 50, 60, 78, 113
Byrnes, James, 44, 45

C

Carter, President Jimmy, 6, 9, 14, 78, 82, 86, 116, 120, 135, 137, 138
Carter's doctrine, 86, 92
casualties, 13, 63, 98

Chechnya, 22
chemical weapons, 30, 110
Churchill, Winston, ix, 43, 44, 47
CIA, 16, 84
Civil War, 14, 125
Clinton administration, 37
Clinton, President Bill, 8, 14, 17, 20, 37, 106, 117, 120, 123, 138
Cold War, ix, 10, 11, 17, 20, 22, 35, 41, 42, 43, 44, 47, 48, 55, 56, 63, 66, 68, 69, 74, 81, 82, 83, 85, 88, 93, 95, 96, 98, 101, 106, 107, 109, 111, 115, 117, 123, 137
collective security alliance, 115
Colombia, 10, 22, 130, 131, 132
Colombian-Panamanian conflict, 11
colonization, 11
combating terror, 104
commander-in-chief, 7, 9, 10, 80
commerce, 28, 36, 38
communism, 42, 49, 52, 53, 62, 63, 66, 74, 82, 83, 88, 89, 90, 92, 98, 100, 102, 104, 109, 111, 115, 116, 123
Constitution, 7, 8, 14, 80
containment, 16, 42, 47, 53, 62-64, 66, 68, 90, 95-99, 115, 116, 123
corruption, 54, 91, 106
Cuba, 4, 10, 84, 102, 103, 130, 131
Cuban Missile Crisis, 10, 97, 115

D

Department of Defense, 16, 33
Department of Homeland Security, 21
domestic policy, 14, 16, 22

E

Economic Cooperation Administration, 52
economic growth, 70, 87, 88, 106
economic interests, 2, 91
economic policy, 103
economic prosperity, 52, 53, 104, 117
economic recession, 91

Eisenhower, President Dwight D., 115, 120
ethnocentrism, 50, 51
executive branch, 62, 80, 110
expansion of territory, 13

F

FBI, 22
FDR/Truman regime, 15, 16, 17, 21, 22
federal budget, 87
federal government, 78, 83
financial assets, 21
First World War, 35
Ford, President Gerald, 9, 69
foreign aid, 33, 43, 52, 53
foreign policy strategy, 57, 74
foreign policy, ix, x, xi, 1, 2, 3, 4, 5, 6, 7, 8, 9, 14, 15, 16, 19, 20, 21, 22, 25, 26, 27, 28, 38, 39, 41, 42, 47, 49, 50, 51, 52, 54, 56, 59, 60, 61, 62, 63, 64, 65, 66, 67, 68, 69, 72, 73, 74, 77, 78, 79, 80, 81, 82, 83, 85, 89, 92, 93, 96, 98, 113, 114, 115, 116, 118, 121, 139
Fourteen Points speech, 25, 27, 30, 38
France, x, 3, 35, 67, 108, 121, 130

G

Germany, x, 3, 35, 42, 43, 44, 97, 108, 125
global security, 32, 35, 37, 86, 87, 90, 91, 93, 139
Grand Alliance, 42, 43, 48
Great Britain, 43, 44, 45, 48, 125
Great White Fleet, 16, 95
Greece, 48, 49, 51, 52, 53, 54, 55, 61, 62, 97, 122, 129
Grenada, 8, 132

H

Hague Conventions, 13
Harding, President Warren G., 20
homeland security, x, 21, 104
humanitarian intervention, 20

I

idealism, 50, 51, 52, 77, 89, 93, 114
ideology, 6, 47, 55, 81, 82, 83, 98
impeachment, 116
inaugural address, 65, 67, 85
inflation, 83, 86, 97
innocents, 13, 51, 105
international affairs, ix, x, 3, 4, 10, 11, 14, 15, 16, 20, 30, 33, 37, 59, 60, 62, 63, 66, 74, 81, 95, 97, 98, 108
international crisis, 62, 63
international environment, ix, 6, 22, 28, 33, 34, 35, 42, 85, 90, 93
international inspection system, 45
International Monetary Fund, 48
international relations, 2, 42, 63, 81, 82, 83, 92, 139
international security, 20, 55
international terrorism, ix, 11, 33, 51, 100, 104, 106, 109, 117
international terrorists, 22
international trade, 27, 28, 32, 34, 36, 103
international treaties, 20, 21
internationalism, 17, 26, 29, 87
investment, 17, 28, 34, 87, 106
Iran-Contra, 110
Iraq, x, 8, 12, 21, 29, 96, 101, 105, 106, 108, 110, 118, 132, 133
iron curtain, 102
Islamic fundamentalism, 53
isolationism, 5, 15, 27, 41, 42, 62
Italy, 42, 125, 129

J

Japan, 30, 42, 43, 44, 45, 46, 60, 107, 125, 128
Jefferson, Thomas, 9, 15, 119, 140
Johnson, President Lyndon B., 9, 63, 115, 120
jus ad bellum, 12, 13
jus in bello, 12, 13
just war, 12, 13

K

Kennedy, John F., 115, 120
Kissinger, Henry, 25, 26, 39, 47, 55, 63, 64, 65, 66, 67, 68, 69, 116, 136
Korea, 8, 63, 83, 84, 97, 105, 106, 107, 108, 128, 129, 136
Kosovo, 8, 10

L

Latin America, 3, 4, 10, 36, 121, 123, 130
law enforcement, 21, 35, 104
League of Nations, 27, 28, 31, 60, 95, 114, 115
legislative branch, 80
legitimacy, 37, 45, 68
liberalism, 52, 54

M

MacArthur, General, 45
Manchuria, 44, 46
manifest destiny, 5, 15
Marshall Plan, 16, 49, 52, 53, 55, 115
Marshall, George, 48, 49, 52
Marxism, 47, 96, 99
Marxist ideology, 47
Mexican-American War, 16
Middle East peace, 21
military assistance, 18, 67, 123
military capability, 37
military force, 4, 7, 9, 10, 11, 12, 18, 21, 55, 71, 86, 88, 90, 91
military power, 10, 29, 35, 41, 47, 97, 101, 104
military tribunals, 21, 22
Molotov, Vyacheslav, 43
Monroe Doctrine, 3, 4, 10, 16, 60, 121
Monroe, President James, ix, 9, 11, 119
moral justness, 12
most favored nation, 9
multilateral agreements, 34
Muslim, 53, 105, 107
mutually assured destruction, 56, 103, 106

N

National Security Council, 16
national security doctrines, xi, 10, 11, 18
national security policy, ix, x, xi, 1, 2, 4, 7, 9, 10, 11, 13, 14, 15, 16, 17, 19, 20, 22, 78, 95
National Security Strategy (NSS), x, xi, 5, 6, 22, 26, 27, 28, 29, 32, 33, 34, 35, 36, 37, 38, 39, 42, 49, 50, 51, 52, 53, 54, 55, 56, 60, 69, 70, 72, 74, 78, 79, 87, 88, 89, 90, 91, 92, 93, 98, 99, 101, 102, 104, 105, 107, 109, 110, 113, 118, 124, 135, 139
Native Americans, 8
Nazi, 44
New Deal, 14
Nixon Doctrine, 59, 62, 64, 65, 66, 67, 68, 72, 73, 74, 115, 123
Nixon, Richard M., 6, 8, 9, 17, 59, 62, 63, 64, 65, 66, 67, 68, 69, 72, 73, 74, 75, 97, 115, 116, 120, 123, 136, 137, 138
non-nuclear aggression, 65
Noriega, 132
North Atlantic Treaty Organization (NATO), x, 16, 28, 29, 34, 101-103, 107, 115, 117, 129
nuclear umbrella, 18, 123
nuclear weapons, 11, 46, 85, 92, 100, 103, 104, 106, 111

O

P

Panama Canal, 11, 16, 60, 85, 102
partisan politics, 57
partisanship, 61
Pentagon, x
People's Republic of China, 9
Persian Gulf, 8, 86, 97, 101, 123, 132
policy agenda, 62
policy goals, 60, 62, 71
policymaking, 12

political advantage, 32
political agenda, 85
political culture, 50
political influence, 37
political parties, 99
Polk, James K., 10, 119
Pompidou, President Georges, 67
Powell, Colin, 18
pre-established treaties, 66
presidential leadership, 8
presidential national security doctrines, xi, 22, 113
presidential power, 14, 16, 19, 22, 60
presidential psychology, 11
proposals, 44, 64, 73, 74, 75
protectionist tariffs, 32
public awareness, 33, 37
public opinion, 92, 105, 108
Puerto Rico, 130

R

radical Islamic groups, 22
Reagan, President, 6, 8, 14, 15, 18, 69, 95-103, 108-111, 116-118, 120, 123, 136, 137, 138
realpolitik, 116
reconstruction, 48, 54
regulations on arms, 31
Republican administration, 37
Republican Party, 20, 46
Revolutionary War, 125
Rice, Condoleezza, 37, 137
Romania, 43, 45, 121
Roosevelt Corollary, 4, 10, 121
Roosevelt, Franklin D. (FDR), x, 14, 15, 16, 17, 20, 21, 22, 42, 52, 60, 114, 120
Roosevelt, President Theodore, 11
Russia, 22, 29, 30, 31, 34, 36, 56, 60, 107, 109, 129
Russo-Japanese War, 11, 16, 128

S

Saudi Arabia, 46, 132

security objectives, 2, 36, 102
Senate, 8, 60, 84
Shultz, George, 18, 19
slavery, 105
Soviet Union, 10, 11, 16, 20, 30, 41, 42, 43, 44, 45, 46, 47, 48, 49, 52, 53, 55, 56, 61, 63, 66, 68, 69, 74, 81, 82, 83, 84, 86, 89, 90, 92, 95, 96, 97, 99, 100, 101, 102, 103, 104, 106, 108, 109, 110, 111, 115, 116, 117, 123, 136, 137
Spanish-American War, 4, 8, 16, 125
spheres of influence, 45
Stalin, Joseph, 42-47
State Department, 46, 107
State of the Union, 78, 79, 85, 86, 88, 92, 102, 123
strategic arms limitation talks (SALT), 68, 83, 84, 90
Strategic Defense Initiative, 103, 108

T

Taliban regime, 21, 133
tariffs, 34
tax policies, 34
terrorism, x, xi, 9, 41, 51, 52, 53, 55, 56, 70, 73, 74, 87, 88, 89, 90, 92, 93, 96, 101, 105, 107, 108, 110, 111
terrorist attacks, ix, 20, 61, 71, 73, 96, 98, 99, 109, 117
terrorist threat, 21, 33, 70, 90
terrorists, 21, 34, 35, 61, 69, 70, 71, 90, 96, 104, 109, 110, 124, 129, 133
trade relations, 34
transformative regime, 14, 15, 19
Truman administration, 42, 43, 44, 46, 47, 48, 50, 52, 53, 54, 55, 56, 57, 115
Truman Doctrine, 47, 49, 50, 52, 53, 54, 56, 61, 62, 115
Truman, President Harry S., 6, 8, 9, 15, 16, 17, 20, 21, 22, 41, 42, 43, 44, 45, 46, 47, 48, 49, 50, 51, 52, 53, 54, 55, 56, 61, 62, 67, 85, 93, 95, 96, 97, 111, 114, 115, 117, 118, 120, 122, 135, 136, 137, 140

Turkey, 44, 45, 46, 49, 52, 54, 55, 61, 62, 97, 122, 129

U

U.S. allies, 20, 62, 70, 71, 100, 123
U.S. foreign policy,, xi, 5
U.S. Navy, 139
UN Security Council, 48
unilateralism, 118
United Nations, x, 16, 28, 31, 36, 43, 45, 95, 115, 117, 118
USSR, 43, 44, 46, 96, 100, 111

V

Vietnam War, 10, 17, 63, 66, 73, 83, 97, 115, 123, 129

W

War of 1812, 8, 125, 132
war on terror, xi, 21, 22, 61, 70, 71, 72, 73, 87, 93, 96, 105, 107, 108, 110, 111
War on Terrorism, 33
war powers, 7
war to end all wars, 30
Warsaw Pact, 101, 104
Washington, George, 3, 7, 8, 59, 60, 75, 119
Watergate, 73, 83, 97, 116
weapons of mass destruction (WMD), 21, 34, 35, 56, 70, 87, 93, 105, 106, 109, 110, 133
Weinberger, 18, 19
Weinberger, Caspar, 18
Western Europe, 46, 49, 53, 115
Wilson, Woodrow, xi, 6, 20, 25-33, 35-39, 60, 93, 93, 95, 113, 114, 118, 120, 121, 136, 137
Wilson's Fourteen Points, 26, 27, 28, 30, 33, 36, 39, 118, 121
Wilsonian beliefs, 37
Wilsonian idealism, 25
World Bank, 48

World Trade Center, x, 69
world view, ix, 6, 22, 122
World War I, 8, 11, 29, 30, 38, 41, 60, 61, 62, 95, 96, 103, 107, 111, 114, 115, 121, 122, 125

World War II, 8, 11, 13, 16, 17, 20, 41, 42, 52, 55, 60-62, 96, 103, 107, 111, 114, 115, 122, 125, 128, 129, 131